How Churches Grow in an Urban World

HOW CHURCHES GROW
IN AN URBAN WORLD

FRANCIS M. DUBOSE

BROADMAN PRESS
Nashville, Tennessee

4225–31

ISBN: 0–8054–2531–4

Dewey Decimal Classification: 254.2

Subject heading: CITY CHURCHES

Library of Congress Catalog Card Number: 78–66 365

Printed in the United States of America

Foreword

It was precisely in the urban context that the church was born. In that setting it has grown, thrived, struggled, and died. In some cases it has had a glorious resurrection from its urban grave. A major purpose of this study is to examine church growth in light of its urban context—biblical, historical, contemporaneous—in an effort to discover the principles of both life and death in the city. We ask the question: What is there about the city which has made it that awesome paradox: both the fertile field for the birth and growth of the church and the grim graveyard for the struggle and death of the church?

To raise this one profoundly complex question is to invite a veritable avalanche of related queries. Why did the early church thrive in its urban context, despite the fact that that context was often hostile? What complementary ingredients exist in the city and the church to cause them to strike up such an affinity? Conversely, what happens in the cities to change the situation so totally and to bring about the demise of thousands of congregations?

A fascinating question relates to the development of the rich variety of congregational types in the city. To what extent does the urban form affect a church type? The very classification of churches reveals the significant influence a particular urban physical setting has upon determining various congregational models: the downtown church, the uptown church, the inner-city church, the neighborhood church, the university church, the suburban church. If the urban *soma* ("body" or form) influences the shape of the congregation, what about the urban *psyche* ("soul" or life)? Do not such types as the people's church, the storefront church, the ethnic church, the house church, the black church strongly suggest the influence of the urban style upon congregational types?

There are three observable attitudes which are institutionalized in an urban society: (1) that which is essentially urban, (2) that which is an adaptation to urbanism from an earlier ruralism, (3) that which is basically a reaction against urbanism. The first identifies with urban heterogeneity (pluralism), the second with the homogeneous primary group within the city, and the third with rural nostalgia. To what extent are the churches in the urban context reflective of these respective attitudes: (1) expressions of, (2) adaptations to, or (3) reactions against the urban psyche? And how does this affect how they grow or why they do not grow? How does this affect whether or not a church is indigenous— natural, normative, and nonalien to its general or local urban context?

A related question probes more deeply into the urban *psyche*. How does the urban way of life affect church life in general and the congregation in particular? What about such basic urban characteristics as massiveness, anonymity, heterogeneity, mobility, conflict, secularization, and change? Does the Bible have anything to say about these urban qualities? If so, what?

What light does the Bible throw upon the city? Is the biblical attitude positive, negative, or mixed? What basic theological principles do we derive from this biblical view of urban life, especially as it relates to the church in the city? Is there any theological significance to the fact that the New Testament records such phenomenal growth of the church in its first century urban context?

What about patterns of urban church growth since then? Is all growth good? What lessons do we learn from the Bible and history concerning the most effective strategy for our day?

One of the most disturbing questions centers on the adverse sometimes fatal effect urban social change has upon the Christian congregation. Why is it that the central city churches have been so vulnerable to these social changes? This leads to an even more fundamental question: What about the transcendent dimension? Is not the church a divine institution as well as a human institution? Why is it that the church behaves more like any other social institution rather than like the divine institution it is supposed to be? Is its human aspect more determinative than its divine aspect of how it fares in its social environment? This reveals the essentially theological nature of the issues we face as we enter our quest for the answer to how churches grow in an urban world.

This book grows out of a deep commitment to the church and church growth and also a real concern for the soundest possible theology and the healthiest possible strategy for that church growth in our emerging urban world. It seeks to address itself, therefore, to the basic areas which many feel are not treated adequately in the current literature on church growth: (1) a clear urban perspective, (2) a balanced theology of growth, (3) a comprehensive strategy, (4) growth for transitional churches.

Of the numerous helpful current studies on church growth, few deal with the urban dimension. Moreover, none struggles with the meaning of the urban way of life and the effect of that urbanism on church life and church growth. Likewise, of the excellent urban church studies which have appeared in recent years, virtually none deals with church growth as such although a number do deal with the general effectiveness of the urban church. This study seeks to bring together the best insights from these areas and wed them in such a way as to speak to recognized problems. Although the work is from a North American perspective primarily, it has been written consciously with the international community in mind, drawing its insights and illustrations from as wide a base as possible. The author therefore hopes that the study will be able to serve the church around the world.

To my wife
DOROTHY ANN SESSUMS DUBOSE
My lover and my best friend

Contents

Introduction: Urgent Needs in Church Growth Studies   11

Part I—Understanding an Urban World
     1. The Emerging Urban World   21
     2. Communication and the Urban Scenario   31

Part II—History: How Churches *Have* Grown
     3. The Urban First Century   43
     4. The Recent Urban Past   58
     5. The Urban Present   75

Part III—Theology: How Churches *Should* Grow
     6. A Theology of the City   100
     7. A Theology of Urbanism   111
     8. Theological Correctives for Healthy Growth   121

Part IV—Strategy: How Churches *Can* Grow
     9. A Comprehensive Approach to Strategy   136
     10. The Inner City: Renewal and New Growth   145
     11. The Growing Edge: Advance on All Fronts   153

Conclusion: Summary of Principles   169

Introduction
Urgent Needs
in Church Growth Studies

Current church growth studies reflect an urgent need for further investigation of the subject from a clear urban perspective. Related to this are other areas that need urgent attention: a balanced theology of growth, a comprehensive approach to strategy, and special help for the transitional church.

The last two decades have witnessed a mounting interest in church growth studies. The Institute of Church Growth and School of World Mission of the Fuller Theological Seminary at Pasadena, California, has been a leader in this movement. Other groups have emerged in the last few years with a strong emphasis on church growth, most of them obviously influenced by the Fuller School. The result has been a growing body of literature dealing with the subject, however, little of it has concentrated on "urban" church growth.

A Clear Urban Perspective

Besides one volume written from a Latin American perspective and a small volume of case studies, all of the recent discussions of urban church growth have been chapters in books or articles in church growth bulletins. Roger Greenway's *An Urban Strategy for Latin America* deals with church growth, but it is a Latin American perspective with Mexico City as his model. His more recent *Guidelines for Urban Church Planting* is the first volume to deal with urban church planting as such. It is a helpful case study approach which illustrates missionary methods of urban church planting by various denominations in seven countries. The introductory chapter, "Keys to Urban Church Planting," is an exposition of Donald McGavran's "Eight Keys to Church Growth in Cities" listed in *Understanding Church Growth*. It is interesting that McGavran and Wayne Weld revise this list and reduce the original eight to "Six Keys to the Cities" in their joint work *Principles of Church Growth* published in 1974.

Several works over the last few years have included chapters dealing in some way with urban church growth. In *Understanding Church Growth*, which appeared in 1970, McGavran includes a chapter on "Discipling Urban Populations." M. Wendell Belew's *Churches and How They Grow*, published in 1971, has three chapters which deal respectively with the growth of city, inner city, and suburban churches. In *Frontiers in Missionary Strategy*, C. Peter Wagner has a chapter on "Strategy for Urban Evangelism" which offers "Six Important Steps in Multiplying Urban Congregations." In his edited work of 1972, *Crucial Issues in Missions Tomorrow*, McGavran features an article by Edward Murphy on "Guidelines for Urban Church Planting." In their joint work of 1974, *How to Grow a Church*, McGavran and Win C. Arn deal with urban church types: "First Church," "Changing Church," "Suburban Church." In another joint venture, alluded to above, McGavran and Weld deal with "The Urban Church" in one of their fifteen chapters. Ezra Earl Jones in *Strategies for New Churches* deals with urban congregations as a part of a larger treatment of general types. Lyle Schaller has dealt in some measure with urban church growth in a number of works which have appeared recently. Two of these are *Planning for Protestantism in Urban America* and *Hey That's Our Church*.

In *Introducing Church Growth: A Textbook for Missions*, Tetsuneo Yamamori and E. LeRoy Lawson have a chapter on "Insights from Behavioral Sciences." In this chapter is a section on "Social Structures, Decision-Making, and Church Growth." They speak of "a sociological scheme which expresses the structural change from a basically agrarian orientation to an industrial-urban one." [1] The authors give seven contrasts under these two categories. However, they neither show how this applies to church growth nor do they cite any work which does. Indeed, there has been none.

The Church Growth Bulletin has had a few helpful articles on urban church growth. The July 1976 issue includes Vergil Gerber's "A New Tool for Winning the City," and the September 1975 issue includes several articles on the subject.

A number of recent books on the urban church have dealt indirectly with the matters of urban church growth. Murray Leiffer's older work, now revised, *The Effective City Church,* is a good example. Of course, most of the works on church growth apply in some way to the urban church.

At first glance the above descriptions might indicate a fair amount of material dealing with urban church have dealt indirectly with the matter of urban church growth. However, when we compare it to the total volume of material on church growth, we discover only a fraction on the urban situation. Moreover, these approaches do not go to the heart of the nature and implications of urban form and life as they relate to historical and contemporary church growth and decline.

The most crucial need is in an urban interpretation. We need to view our biblical, historical, and contemporary sources from an urban perspective. What does this data tell us about how urban reality has influenced church growth? How has urban form helped to determine the method and style of church growth and life? How has urbanism affected church growth? How has church growth been affected by the basic characteristics of the urban way of life: massiveness, anonymity, heterogeneity, mobility, conflict, secularization, change? These fundamental questions must be faced if we are to understand urban church growth.

A Balanced Theology of Growth

The theological studies on church growth are quite limited. *Church Growth and Christian Mission,* edited by McGavran and published in 1965, deals with "Theological Issues." The three chapters in this section give a good general theological rationale for church growth, but they do not speak to some of the more crucial biblical and theological issues which have been raised in the last decade. In *God, Man, and Church Growth,* edited by

A. R. Tippett, Arthur F. Glasser has a chapter on "Church Growth and Theology." It deals with general biblical principles which form the basis for church growth. With regard to biblical material, Tippett's *Church Growth and the Word of God* provides helpful material on the biblical concept of growth. Harvie M. Conn's *Theological Perspectives on Church Growth* is more of a methodology than a theology. However, his chapter on "God's Plan for Church Growth: An Overview" is a helpful general survey of church growth principles in the Bible.

These and other church growth studies have met a deep need, and enthusiasm for the movement has spread rapidly over the past few years. However, there has also been a growing widespread dissatisfaction with some emphases in the church growth movement. This has been due largely to what some feel is the lack of a "holistic" or balanced approach, especially by the Fuller School. Orlando Costas has perhaps given the most articulate critique of the weaknesses of the church growth movement.

Costas praises the church growth movement for the positive role it has played in its challenge to the missionary enterprise, in its insight into conversion, evangelism, and church growth, and in its stimulation of the study of mission. However, he faults it for basically one reason, its imbalance. In demonstrating this, he examines critically what he feels is its limitation in its principles of interpretation, its view of mission, its view of man, and its methodology as well as its theology. Basic to his critique is what he calls a "questionable theological *locus.*" This *locus* is a church-centered theology. This is questionable, Costas feels, because the *locus* of a biblical theology should focus on Christ, his kingdom, and his redemptive work in the world. It should not make the church an end within itself, as he feels church growth theology tends to do.[2] While Costas has perhaps been the most vocal critic, statements from other Christian quarters seem to object to a decidedly one-sided view of church growth.

McGavran and the Fuller School have made an enormous contribution to missiology in their use of anthropology to complement biblical insight. However, some feel that where there is conflict between the two, anthropology seems to prevail over theology. The church growth theory at times seems to be basically an anthropological pragmatism with a kind of biblical rationale surrounding it.

This pragmatism is the result of what many feel is an overemphasis on quantity. Let it be accented strongly that quantitative or numerical growth is important. It was important to Luke as the book of Acts plainly reveals, and it must be important to us. Indeed the future of Christianity hangs upon the healthy numerical growth of churches. As important as numerical growth is, however, to be completely preoccupied with it, results in the neglect of qualitative growth which is an unhealthy position from a biblical perspective. Moreover, to assume that qualitative growth always attends quantitative growth is not to come to terms with reality.

While it is necessary to test current church growth principles theologically and to bring the searchlight of Scripture to bear upon them, it is much more important to establish a positive theological approach for the understanding of church growth, especially in the urban context. A sound biblical theology of urban church growth must first examine what the Bible says about the city and then examine the meaning of urbanism in light of the Scriptures. It then should examine those principles of growth which were obvious in the spread of the New Testament church in its urban context. Out of this will come the healthy, balanced view of growth relevant to our emerging urban age.

The value of the above critique is in the fact that Costas himself is committed to church growth. He therefore speaks sympathetically. Yet he seeks to be objective as he offers both positive and negative evaluations of the church growth movement. As a Third World evangelical, he brings insights which North-Atlantic mission strategists would do well to heed.

To the credit of the Fuller School, it should be emphasized that it has encouraged dialogue on church growth principles which it has been compelled to recognize as controversial. C. Peter Wagner of Fuller has written one of the forewords for Costas' book.

Donald McGavran, in his *Eye of the Storm: The Great Debate in Mission,* incorporates in his work a number of essays which take issue with his position.

Recognizing the controversial nature of the "homogeneous unit principle" (see chapter 8), the Fuller School hosted a major dialogue session on the subject sponsored by the Lausanne Theology and Educational Group in May and June of 1977. Five faculty members of Fuller presented position papers on the principle and five discussants, all leading theologians, prepared responses to these. Again, the value of this is in the fact that both sides are committed to church growth. The ten men debated the subject with the aid of twenty-five leading contemporary theologians.

We have everything to gain from such enlightened discussion of contemporary church growth theory and practice. This study is a part of that continuing dialogue, and the ideas set forth here are intended to be both constructive evaluations of church growth principles and a sincere call to fill the unmet needs in church growth studies which cry out to us.

A Comprehensive Strategy

The pragmatic nature of current church growth theory has left us vulnerable to a kind of gimmickry of instantism. Quick results in one area only with a virtual oblivion to the total cause and to the total issues of the faith is not the answer. As we face our urban future, we need a sound and comprehensive strategy for church growth based upon biblical principles and all the historical and contemporary insight we can gather tested by those biblical principles.

This comprehensive strategy should plan for a healthy, balanced growth. As we anticipate this growth, there are three basic frames of reference to guide us: (1) organic and influential growth, (2) enlargement and multiplication growth, (3) qualitative and quantitative growth. The church is an organism and therefore should grow as a living entity: enlarging, expanding, extending, multiplying. It is also the instrument of God's glory and should cause the spread of that glory as a witness over the earth. The growth of Christian influence complements the growth of the church organism. The church should thrive and flourish as a single congregation itself, but it should also reproduce itself. Giving birth to other churches should be as much a part of its nature as to grow itself as a church. The enlargement of existing churches and the planting of new churches go hand in hand in the spread of the faith. At the same time, a vital part of any growth situation is growth in quality. We are to grow in wisdom as well as stature. This is no less true for the church. Qualitative and quantitative growth are both a part of God's desire for his church, and one should never be emphasized at the expense of the other.

If we are to implement a comprehensive strategy, it will call for cooperation at every possible level. There must be cooperation within the larger Christian community. Sharing across denominational lines is necessary. Interchurch and parachurch groups have much to share with each other. The Fuller School has led the way in providing training and producing studies which have benefitted many church groups and missions. Cooperation between schools, research centers, and other avenues of expertise is needed for maximum effectiveness in planning for church growth in our urban future.

A fuller and more integrated strategy needs to be developed within denominations. Every entity within a denomination has much at stake in church growth. It is basic to all that we do, and all we shall be able to do in the future. Indeed, the extent and nature of church growth is crucial to the determination of our future. A fuller cooperation between churches at the local denominational level is absolutely necessary if there is to be an effective strategy of church growth for any given urban area.

Special Help for the Transitional Church

A major casualty of the urban revolution has been the inner city. It is difficult to over emphasize the seriousness of this problem. The term *inner city* is essentially sociological though its implication is spatial or geographic. It refers to the transitional residential area traditionally near the central and secondary business districts of the city. Its primary application is to North America. The British speak of the "city centre" referring essentially to the same thing conveyed by the more North American term *inner city.*

The inner-city church has been a part of this casualty of urban social change. The term *inner city* now refers to any transitional area of an urban center, whether or not it is located in the geographic inner city. Though the inner city in the United States has unique features because of the uniqueness of American sociology, the crisis of the church in the "city centre" in Britain is strikingly similar to the crisis of the church in the inner city of the United States. They are both victims of a drastic transition. The inner city has always been the home of slums and other undesirable aspects of urban society, but the problem of the inner city today is far greater than its slums and its skid rows. It is the problem of a critical transition which is affecting the lives of millions of people and thousands of churches. The crux of the problem is that Christian congregations, which once thrived in stable, middle-class urban communities, now find themselves surrounded by social change so profound that it has rendered their communities unrecognizable in terms of their constituency and the general social climate of the area. The change in the North American city has been especially acute because of the seriousness and complexity of the social crisis which has been vividly dramatized in the theater of the inner city.

The mechanization of farming rendered the tenant farmer obsolete and sent the poor to the inner city in search of survival. The same revolutionary process provided the technology which has made the urban middle class increasingly affluent and has sent it to the more affluent suburbs. The older city housing, which has been abandoned by the middle class and its children, has been left for the incoming poor and unskilled who have neither the means nor the motivation to maintain it. Thus almost overnight, once stable urban residential areas have been and are being transformed into transitional communities. In some cases it has taken two or three decades; in others, two or three years.

The inability of the inner-city church to cope with this change has brought the greatest crisis to the Christian congregation in the history of the American church. Many of these churches have died. Many have merged. Many have moved. In a fifteen-year-period just after World War II, fifty-three mainline Protestant churches moved from the central area of Detroit. Many still struggle to survive in their changed and changing context.

The impact of this phenomenon has been catastrophic. It has meant the death or decline of thousands of congregations in the United States. This has resulted not only in a significant loss of churches, but it has had a grave psychological effect upon church life in general. Moreover, it has had international repercussions. Congregational church models around the world have been increasingly influenced by the models of North America from which the growing support has come for the mission enterprise around the world. If we can determine why churches have declined in the wake of this social change and if we can deal adequately with these reasons, it will serve us well in our urban future.

Notes

[1] (Cincinnati: A Division of Standard Publishing, 1975), p. 81.

[2] Orlando Costas, *The Church and Its Mission: A Shattering Critique from the Third World* (Wheaton, Ill.: Tyndale House Publishers, Inc., 1974), pp. 123–49.

Part I

Understanding an Urban World

1 The Emerging Urban World

Today we stand at the threshold of an urban world. Urban reality has been with us since the dawn of civilization, but today mankind is being enveloped in a social process in which urban reality pervades the totality of existence. Harvard theologian Harvey Cox has said that "future historians will record the twentieth century as that century in which the whole world became one immense city." [1]

The Urbanization of Man

The city is the supreme symbol of civilization—indeed, the city is civilization. The cities of history and the civil orders which they built paralleled the nomad and village cultures from which they came. From time to time these different cultural expressions met and clashed. Today they are being fused into a new form of urbanism which promises to be the essential life-style of mankind for the foreseeable future. Stubborn nostalgic trends may appear and reappear. Nevertheless, this urban process is so pronounced in its character that it is proving to be both inevitable and irreversible.

We have moved in the process of history from the first advent of the urban phenomenon, to the emergence of urban man as a distinct type in contrast to nomad man and village man, finally to the beginning of the process which will witness the essential urbanization of mankind. This urban reality is reflected in the very titles of definitive studies which have appeared recently. [2]

The Great Urban Waves of History

Because most of the patterns of contemporary urbanism are inherited from the urban past, it will be helpful to survey briefly the significant stages in the history of urbanization. There have been four great urban waves in history. The first began around 5000–6000 B.C. and lasted until around A.D. 500, the general date for the fall of Rome. This ancient city or town *(polis)* developed from the small village. Except for giants such as Rome, the ancient city would resemble in size our towns of today. The features of the first urban expression were religion which was symbolized by the temple, commerce which was symbolized by the market, defense which was symbolized by the garrison, and politics which was symbolized by the palace. Some characteristic ancient cities were Jericho, Byblos, Jerusalem, Babylon, Nineveh, Persepolis, Athens, Sparta, and Rome.

After the fall of Rome, Western civilization reverted to an essentially village pattern. A half millenium later the *polis* was revived, and a second urban wave emerged. The force which gave rise to this *neopolis* (new city) was the Renaissance. The same ancient institutions continued to characterize city life: religion, commerce, defense, and politics. There were some new features in this period, however: the invention of the printing press, the stratification of art, the rise of the university, the development of urban legal innovations, and the emergence of an incipient middle class. Characteristic cities of the *neopolis* were Rome, Bologna, Florence, Constantinople, London, Paris, Toledo (Spain).

The third great urban wave began around 1800. It was characterized by rapid industrial development. Cities developed to such an unprecedented size that they reached out and enveloped the surrounding villages. This was the beginning of suburban development in the modern sense. The industrial city became the *metropolis,* the "mother-city," the large central city surrounded by suburban satellite communities. This urban era was marked by the development of large corporations, a concentration of a country's wealth and political power in the urban centers, and the development of intricate social specialization. In this era mass communication reached an unprecedented stage of development through the printed page, the radio, the movies, and the beginning of television. This period of urban development produced an authentic middle class which for the first time in history became the majority population in the industrialized countries. Characteristic cities of this era are the great urban giants: New York, Chicago, London, Berlin, Paris, Tokyo, Moscow.

The last great urban wave began around the close of World War II. It grew out of the Industrial Revolution which lasted into this century. This urban wave is characterized by the technological revolution. It is the era of the *megalopolis,* "the great city."

Admittedly the above historical survey is from the perspective of Western civilization. It should be emphasized, however, that the non-Western world has had urban civilizations which go back hundreds and even thousands of years. Asia, especially China and India, the Americas, and Africa have had very sophisticated cities from times of antiquity.

The So-called "Urban Exodus"

A recent development in the United States has evoked some interesting speculation. It has been reported that now in the United States the urban trend has been reversed and people are moving back to the country. We must not be fooled by this so-called "urban exodus." Who are these people who are making their getaway and are occupying these nonurban areas? Urbanites all. More correctly "rurbanites." They certainly are not swelling the ranks of the farming populations. That figure has dropped from around 25 percent in 1930 to around 4 percent today.[3] It continues to drop each year.

It is true that as a part of the general nostalgic trend, a number of people are moving to once declining rural areas and therefore reversing the declining population trend in some of those sections. These urban escapees may be classified as: (1) the prosperous retired and semiretired, (2) the mobile affluent professional and vocational specialist or expert, (3) the long-distance commuter, (4) the "would-be farmer" with some other source of income, (5) a few new farmers who are not sufficient in number to compensate for those who quit each year, (6) the people who serve those who are mentioned above.

The great majority of these people are not going back to farms, certainly not to a farm culture. They are still essentially urbanites, that special brand we now call "rurbanites."

They live in the country but are connected in some way to the economy of an urban center. They maintain an essentially urban life-style, living in houses with most if not all the modern conveniences, watching TV, driving an automobile and probably two, doing what most other urbanites do except perhaps garden a little (and a lot of city folks are doing that these days). Although they are able to escape the density of the urban geography, they do not usually escape the "density" of the urban sociology. Some of them are perhaps among that very small minority of "marginal" people in our modern urban society, but most of them are forced in some way to order their lives in response to the dictates of an urban style in which the world of multiple stimuli ultimately prevails.

The Modern Urban Period

Modern society is unmistakably urban, but the shape and style of this modern urbanity have features unknown in the urban expressions of the past. The form of the megalopolis may be viewed from two basic perspectives: the single urban giant or the metropolitan region. The "megacity" of today is far more than a metropolis, mother city with her children satellites. It is that plus a whole region controlled by that center. This includes many smaller cities, towns, villages, and vast rural regions.

In addition to the megalopolis as a vast, single urban center and its region, it also takes the form of a series of metropolitan regions. The particular shape may be linear, multiple, or circular.

The most common shape is linear. Thus the megalopolis in one sense means "strip city." The strip may be viewed both in moderate and vast dimensions. More moderate examples would be illustrated by Dallas-Fort Worth, Seattle-Tacoma, and Los Angeles-San Diego. A classic example of the vast strip city would be the complex and urban giant form which extends from Portland,

Maine to Norfolk, Virginia, with such cities as Washington, New York, Philadelphia in between.

The term *megalopolis* is also used in the sense of a longer and wider strip, connecting smaller strip, cluster, and circular conurbations. An example of this in California is the Los Angeles-San Diego-San Francisco Bay area-Sacramento area with smaller urban regions tying the giants together (Bakersfield, Fresno, Stockton, etc.).

In addition to the more common strip city, there is also the cluster city. This is simply a large expression of a metropolitan giant. An excellent example of this is the greater Los Angeles area which some have referred to as a hundred suburbs in search of a city. The circular city is usually formed around a bay such as the San Francisco Bay where the city links with the South, East, and North bay cities and their satellites to form a vast urban giant of four million people. This form of "the great city" may be seen in varying sizes and shapes in Europe, Asia, Latin America, and even Africa.

In addition to the above, the form or shape of the megalopolis may also be viewed from the standpoint of the social geography of each major urban region. The city as megalopolis has given us a much more complex expression than the city as metropolis which was essentially an urban-suburban phenomenon. A major development in the modern urbanization has been decentralization. The central and secondary business districts of major cities continue to grow as administrational and office centers. Witness the vast downtown development within the last few years of older cities such as San Francisco and younger cities such as Houston. However, their function as a retail outlet has been significantly reduced in recent years. That function is now being assumed by the vastly expanding suburban areas exploding around the rim of the central cities.

The modern era has witnessed the greatest suburban development in history. In the United States more people live in the suburbs than any other form of domicile. Suburbanism has become the norm in American living. A hundred years ago, the typical American family was the rural family. Fifty years ago it was the small town family. Today it is the suburban family.

As suburbia became more and more the norm, its image as a status symbol became tarnished. As the suburbs grew to embrace the lower as well as the upper middle class, affluent suburban pockets emerged quite distinct from the larger middle-class community. Some now refer to this highly affluent aspect of suburbia as "exurbia." These very affluent exurbias may exist farther out beyond the larger suburban communities, but not always. However, they are always distinguished by their highly affluent character.

Added to exurbia is the previously alluded to "rurbia." Actually the term *rurbia* may refer to any aspect of rural transfer or hangover which is apparent in the urban life-styles of modern urban man: recreationalism, retreatism, country domicile, rural motifs in business and entertainment, and nostalgia in general.

The social geography of the megalopolis therefore is far more elaborate than the city and its suburbs. It is made up of a number of distinct parts. The first is "urbia," the central and secondary business districts surrounded by the inner city which is increasingly transitional and which still essentially houses the poor and minorities. The second is "suburbia" which contains the majority middle classes. The third is "exurbia," which houses the elite. The fourth is that interesting and socially diverse company of urban expatriates who now reside outside the geographical and political city in the area we are calling "rurbia."

The city therefore is more than a "place." It is a way of life. It is a state of mind. That mentality may be either positive or negative with varying perspectives within each major mentality. That is, people living in some form of the city are being influenced or perhaps controlled by the urban life-style and are essentially for or against it. Some people love every minute of it; some hate every minute of it. And there are some who are able to adapt and who fall somewhere in between these two extreme attitudes. Some people are very downtown-minded. Others have profound self-images of themselves as suburbanites. Some urbanites who work in the city and play in the country or who have both city and country homes look upon themselves as country gentlemen. They do not want to be identified with the peasant stereotype of the country person. This attitude is urbane as well as urban. The prototype of this rurbanite, of course, goes back to British elitism. On the other hand, many a city person with a strong rural background will always see himself as a country person at heart.

Suburbia, exurbia, and rurbia are therefore more than geography. They are a mentality as well. When we combine these antiurban social-geographies with the antiurban attitude of many who reside within urbia, in the ghettos and elsewhere, we are able to see the plight of the megalopolis as the "city against itself." As the social division in North American society shifted from urban-rural to urban-suburban and came to be contained within the megalopolis itself, and as the "suburban mentality" expanded to include exurbia and rurbia, the megalopolis came to be both city and "anti-city" in one complex and divided whole. The city as a state of mind affects the very style of both urban life in general and urban church life in particular.

The above picture reflects the Western European and North American urban scene of today. The developing nations may not have the same complex variety of social life, but their style is increasingly urban because of the vast urban development which they have experienced in recent years.

Today both East and West are enveloped in a great urban indus-trial-technological development which had its original impetus in the West, even though parts of the East are now as highly developed technologically as the West. Over half of the larger cities in the world are outside the Western world and the so-called developed nations. In the top twenty-five are these fifteen cities: Tokyo, Buenos Aires, Shanghai, Calcutta, Bombay, Peking, Cairo, Rio de Janeiro, Tientsin, Sao Paulo, Osaka, Mexico City, Seoul, Djakarta, Delhi.

Despite the significant differences between urbanization in the

Western and Third Worlds, there are many common aspects. Though the poor are in the minority in the developed nations and in the majority in the undeveloped and developing nations, all nations have their poor. The emerging megalopolis around the world is the place where this reality is sculptured in dramatic relief. Slums and transitional communities plague the modern urban scene the world over. They may be in the inner cities of North America and out on the urban fringes in Africa, Asia, and South America—but they are still slums. They pose the same threat to life and the same challenge to the church.

Urbanism is the same the world over. It knows no nationality, race, economics, politics, religion. When people exist in certain degrees of density, inevitably urbanism becomes a way of life. As urban centers grow larger, there is the constant threat of urban overkill. The modern urban revolution has brought in its wake the intensification of all the traditional urban attributes. Mass becomes even more massive, anonymity even more impersonal, variety even more complex, and movement even more accelerated.

The challenge of the megalopolis is not simply the challenge of an expanding geography. It is the challenge of an overtaxed psyche, with all the attitudinal problems that can arise as a by-product. This urban challenge is a world challenge, but it is especially acute in those parts of the world where urban life has brought its usual problems but few of its usual amenities. Keeping up with the megalopolis will mean, first of all, establishing lines of communication with the people. Nothing can be done until we are on the same wave length with them—both persons and the masses.

Two Significant Facts

There are two supremely significant facts about the modern urban revolution. The first is that the world will soon witness the great majority of its citizens living in or near great urban centers. The process is more pronounced in some countries than others, but there is no country in which this process is not developing to a significant degree. The second significant fact is that all people everywhere are increasingly coming under the dominance of the urban centers and the influence of the urban way of life. This is virtually true now, but the process will be complete in the foreseeable future through the combined technology of communication, transportation, and politics, if not immediately through direct industrial and economic development. Already such people as the great nomad tribe of the Masai of Eastern-Central Africa, who once roamed freely with their cattle over thousands of miles, are now restricted to certain areas and are forced to pay taxes to their city-controlled governments.

The Direction: Ultimate and Irreversible

The city today is so important that the very name of the capital city symbolizes the country itself. When the media reports that Washington speaks or that Moscow speaks, it means that the official word of the government of that country has spoken. Today the city is the point of political power, the matrix of mass media, the origination and destination of the transportation system, the laboratory of the social revolution, the nerve center of society.

In *Man and His Urban Environment,* Fred Smith says:

The city, whether anyone likes it or not, is the natural habitat of civilized man. For every Henry David Thoreau who enjoys living alone in a shed beside a pond, contemplating the infinite wisdom of nature, there are tens of millions who must by some secret but inescapable evolutionary command rub shoulders with their fellowmen, their neighbors, even if they aren't particularly fond of them. It is an instinct we brought with us down through the ages, and it accounts in a large measure for the growth of cities and the emigration, particularly of the young, from the theoretically more desirable smaller centers. *People want to be where the action is.* This is an immensely important consideration, because there is a large body of contemporary opinion that man does not really like cities—and cities are not good for man—and therefore a reasonable solution is to create small towns for people to retreat to, to depend upon these to absorb the population explosion. Such a program on a massive scale is doomed to failure, if only because most men are not like that.[4]

Notes

[1] Harvey Cox, "Mission in a World of Cities," *International Review of Mission,* July, 1966, p. 273.

[2] Some examples are Kingsley Davis, "The Urbanization of the Human Population," *Scientific American* Sept., 1965, and Thelma A. Baker, *The Urbanization of Man: A Social Science Perspective* (Berkeley, CA.; McCutchen Publishing Co., 1972).

[3] *Statistical Abstract of the United States.* (Washington D. C.: U. S. Department of Commerce, Bureau of the Census, 1976), p. 631.

[4] Fred Smith, *Man and His Environment: A Manual of Specific Considerations of the Seventies and Beyond* (Rockefeller Plaza, New York: Man and His Urban Environment Project, 1972), p. 2.

2 Communication and the Urban Scenario

In order to understand urban society, it is necessary to understand how communication takes place in that context. The great communication revolutions of history have been an essential part of the great urban waves of history.

Urbanism and Communication

The phenomenon of "mass" is the first ingredient of the city. The city appears in any circumstance of the historical process when the population develops to the point where sheer mass renders it no longer possible for people to communicate personally so far as their normative public life is concerned.

The City as Communication

Inherent in mass society is the phenomenon of mass communication. Therefore some workable structure of mass communication—understood, accepted, and utilized—is as much a part of mass society as the society itself. Otherwise no society exists—just a mob which can only ultimately destroy itself either by violence or by diffusion into unrelated primary societal units.

Significantly, however, personal and primary group relationships continue in mass society. They are as necessary for psychological, social, and spiritual functioning in an urban society as mass relationships are necessary for economic, political, educational, and other functioning in that society. Communication therefore continues to be a personal and group expression as well as a mass expression in urban society. The significant difference between a rural society and an urban society is that an urban society has the added dimension of mass as an essential element of ordered social life. Out of this phenomenon of mass emerge the numerous features which have come to characterize modern urban society.

Mass Society/Mass Communication

The sheer reality of the development of population beyond a certain point within a limited geographical base necessitates a new way of communication. Out of this comes a new pattern of social order. Louis Wirth, the renowned University of Chicago urban sociologist, wrote in 1938 his classical essay on "Urbanism as a Way of Life." He defines the city "as a relatively large, dense, and permanent settlement of socially heterogeneous individuals." He sees three major sociological realities which characterize the city: (1) numbers of population, (2) density of settlement, (3) heterogeneity or variety of inhabitants and group life.[1] These ingredients necessitate certain patterns of social expression and thus create the urban life-style.

The first reality of urbanism is the phenomenon of "mass," seen in both "numbers of population" and "density of settlement." Wirth therefore saw the whole world of urbanism growing out of the sheer fact of numbers and density. When there is an increase in population within definite geographical limits thus creating density, the city inevitably develops and consequently an urban way of life. Heterogeneity is present from the beginning for the simple reason that people migrate to the city from previously isolated areas. Thus from the beginning there is a difference in culture within the urban expression. If there is the same language, there is a difference in dialect or accent. Domestic and community mores vary, depending upon the village or rural area from which the new urbanites have come. The migration is usually in groups (not always at once, of course). Therefore from the beginning, stratification emerges in urban life, the difference in the groups ranging from mild to sharply contrasting.

The Place of the Personal

Within the city, individuals are usually able to continue primary and personal relationships through homogeneous groups which are either transfers from the former rural and village areas or are newly constructed entities based upon these models. At the same time, however, the newly arrived urbanites must also develop a life-style which relates to the public institutions of mass society of which they are now an essential part.

Even though homogeneity exists within the city, the city as city is heterogeneous, made up of many differing homogeneous groups. Therefore the normative social patterns of urban institutional life result from the intricate interplay between population density and heterogeneity.

Georg Simmel, in his classic essay "The Metropolis and Mental Life," [2] locates the difference between rural and urban societies at the point of stimulus. Rural society is a society of simple stimuli. Urban society by contrast is one of multiple stimuli. In the simple rural context one is able to handle personally all the social stimuli which confront him. In the urban context, however, one is unable to handle personally all the social stimuli which confront him. It is not simply psychologically difficult, it is physically impossible. There are too many people ("numbers of population"); they are too close together ("density of inhabitants"); they exist in too great a variety ("heterogeneity of inhabitants and group life"). As simple stimuli were the norm of simple rural societies of the past, so multiple stimuli is the norm of the complex urban societies of today. Multiple stimuli are inherent in the massive nature of urban life.

Also inherent in this dynamics of massiveness is movement. Wirth emphasizes that both physical footlooseness and social mobility have always characterized urban life. Mobility and change become social necessities emerging out of the dynamics of massiveness of form and life as well as the multiple stimuli which it generates.

From the standpoint of the total social structure of urban life, therefore, patterns of secondary relationships become normative. There are too many people existing in too close a proximity, expressing themselves in too great a variety, and moving too rapidly to permit primary relations to prevail. The only alternative is the creation of mass structures at every area of life, if life is to become functional. This is exactly what has happened in the historical development of cities and urban societies. In this day of the megalopolis characterized by urban diffusion and decentralization, what is lacking in the stimulus of population density is compensated for in the accelerated and intensified stimuli of communication, transportation, and other aspects of our very complex modern style of life.

In order to see more clearly these patterns of the urban expression and other expressions which are inherent in them, the following idealized contrast between the rural and the urban might prove helpful.

RURAL	URBAN
Community Orientation	Society Orientation
Proto-type: the Home	Prototype: the Corporation
Population Sparsity	Population Density
Individual Orientation	Mass Orientation (Organizational Society)
Simple Social Stimuli	Multiple Social Stimuli
Direct Relationships	Indirect (Bureaucratic) Relationships
Primary Relationships	Secondary Relationships
Personal Relationships	Impersonal Relationships
Social Solidarity	Social Change
Sacral Mystique	Secular Attitude
Communal Orientation	Rational Orientation
Emotional-Subjective-Spiritual Mood	Pragmatic-Objective-Utilitarian Mood
Traditional Motivation	Existential (Now) Motivation
Social Integration	Social Stratification
Social Wholeness	Social Segmentalization
Institutional Simplicity	Social Sophistication
Social Homogeneity	Social Heterogeneity
Cooperation	Competition
Harmony, Tranquillity	Conflict, Tension
Occupational Uniformity (Agricultural)	Occupational Specialization (Industrial-Technological)
Immobility	Mobility

Social Isolation	Social Awareness
Economic Independence (Relative)	Economic Interdependence
Non/Semi Money Economy	Complete Money Economy
Social Unity (Residence, Work, Play)	Social Diversity
Social and Emotional Significance of Place	Social Insignificance of Place as Such (Relative)
Residential Community	Trans-Residential Community

A significant fact to understand is that whereas in simple rural life, personal, primary, and direct social relations exist in all areas of life, both public and private—in complex urban life, they exist only in the private sphere. Thus the urbanite, while maintaining some semblance of personal and group life, is forced to pattern the public participation of his life in keeping with the massive structures of urban life, if he is to function normatively in that urban life.

The Evolution of Mass Communication

From the very emergence of mass society, urban man has found ways to structure patterns of mass communication which were indigenous to the genius of the urban life-style.

The Ancient City and the Mass Public Meeting

The first structure of mass communication, which developed as an indigenous expression of communication within the *polis,* was the "public meeting." When the first settlements of civilization developed beyond simple villages into embryonic cities, the need for mass communication developed. Mass communication was as much a cause as an effect of urbanism. The movement from village to city was precisely at the point where the size of the population necessitated mass communication. In and around the life of the first institutions of urban man—the temple, the market, the fort, the palace—the first mass communication emerged. Earlier, more primitive nomad and rural societies had such structures of communication as a chain of drums where simple messages (usually warnings) were relayed to significant numbers of people. However, as important as this system was for these primitive societies, their design was very simple and extremely limited as a communication system. "The public meeting" which emerged in the first cities carried complex messages related to the larger issues of total community life.

Manipulation is common to all forms of communication. However, there is a profound difference between the manipulative principle of communication in the tribal village and that in an urban society. Because communication is structured within a primary group situation in village life, it is automatic. However, because it is structured within a mass context in urban society, it can never be automatic. The leaders in an urban society must earn the right to control.

When urban life developed beyond the simple needs of worship, marketing, and protection, the political sphere developed into greater complexity. In many ancient cities, the palace and the temple were closely aligned, if not united (this was true of the ancient "agri-cities" of the Egyptians and the Incas and Mayas of the Americas). In time, however, they were separated, and the network of public meetings expanded. Later, leisure-oriented cultural developments gave rise to the theater, the coliseum, the hippodrome (race track), and other forms of recreation and pleasure. All of these were structures of mass communication.

Two major types of mass communication in ancient cities were (1) the mass rallies in which rulers shared information of many varieties with their subjects, and (2) the great urban processions such as those leading out to and returning from war. Through all of these structures both "emotion" and "message" were communicated to large numbers of persons at one time. While individuals continued the personal and group relationships which they had always known, they also participated in this mass identity as extensions of themselves and their smaller groups. Without this mass identity and the mass communication which resulted from it, life would have been hopelessly fragmented. Indeed there could have been no cities, no urban societies. This is the reason one of the major concerns of ancient Rome was to control her masses. The mob instinct in the masses which is always just under the surface is a living threat to the order of the city.

The Renaissance City and the Printed Page

The early part of the second great urban wave witnessed the same patterns of communication which prevailed in the period of the ancient city. In the heart of this period, however, one significant achievement brought a totally new dimension to civilization and helped shape the city into a new kind of human experience. It was the invention of the printing press.

The written word has always had great significance. In the pre-Gutenberg era, even though books had to be copied by hand, the written word served as one of the most powerful influences in history. Witness the sacred books of all major religions, the Greek and Roman classics, the early church fathers, and the Renaissance writers. With the invention of movable type, however, history entered a new era.

The appearance of the printing press made it possible to multiply the communication potential of man to degrees so great that the result was no less than revolutionary. It brought not simply a revolution in communication; it brought a revolution in the very mentality and life-style of man. The most significant fact emerging from this new development, of course, was the accessibility of vast amounts of literature to the average person. This was a reality heretofore unknown in the history of mankind. The Renaissance and the literary movements which it influenced, including the Reformation, created a wealth of ideas. The printing press made these ideas and earlier ones available to the average person in vast quantities.

The Industrial City and the Literate Masses

However, it took another great urban wave to create the necessary complement to the printing press. The Industrial Revolution and the urbanization which intensified in its wake created a significant middle class and a consequent unprecedented development in literacy in the Western world. These three history-shaping facts—the Renaissance, the printing press, the Industrial Revolution—combined to produce not only a new city but a new civilization. They released a new energy for political power—an unprecedented participation of the average person in the political process. Today we are still feeling the impact and effect of these significant developments.

There are some five mass media through which the printing press has made its influence felt as a shaper of history: (1) the book, (2) the tract, (3) the newspaper, (4) the periodical, (5) the comic. The first printed material completed by Gutenberg was a book, the most influential of all books—the Bible. The book has a significant influence on urban societies. For example, the numbers of books sold in the United States each year far exceeds the total population, and the per capita sales of volumes in England exceeds that of the United States. The paperback innovation has revolutionized the book industry and has greatly multiplied the accessibility of books to the general public. The tract or pamphlet has been a powerful propaganda tool in the modern political process. Styles of tracts range from Milton's classical works to those by semiliterates, but all styles have their impact. Wisely used tracts have been and still are a meaningful tool of Christian witness.

The daily newspaper is as much an urban institution as the city government, and many urbanites would no more miss their morning newspaper than their breakfast. Periodicals have a wider range of circulation than the newspaper and thus extend their influence over a greater number of people than newspapers. Over twenty-five thousand periodicals ranging from those of wide appeal to those of specialized interest are published weekly and monthly in the United States.

Comics are an often overlooked form of mass communication. They exist in basically four categories: (1) the funny type, (2) the adventure type, (3) the educational or classic type, (4) the horror type. Biblical and Christian comic are now being produced with some success and would fall into category 3 or perhaps 2.

An example of the influence of comics may be illustrated from the fact that over one hundred million copies of comics are printed in the United States monthly and that over 95 percent of the boys and 91 percent of the girls in the United States read them regularly.[3] An example of the potential of the comic strip is seen in the popularity of "Peanuts," which is now having its influence felt in many circles internationally. Through the printed page, the "town crier" has multiplied himself almost without limit. A significant fact that should be observed at this point is that while the printing press has added these significant forms of mass media to the communication network of urban life, the early forms of "the public meeting" continue in greater numbers, in larger proportions, and in new varieties.

The Technological City and the Electronic Media

The three electronic media most significantly affecting modern urban life are: (1) the radio, (2) the movie, (3) the television. These indigenous forms of communication in the modern "technopolis" are altering the shape of modern life. Therefore, no serious discussion of any phase of human endeavor can afford to neglect the careful study of the overwhelming potential for good and evil offered by these life-shaping instruments of mass communication.

Through a newspaper or a periodical one is able to read about an event after he has attended it and thus reexperience it. Or one may read about it and thus experience it by proxy. However, through radio one is able to experience an event by proxy, not later as with a newspaper, but while it is actually transpiring. Moreover, he does it not simply with his eyes, but with his ears, with all the added emotion and rapport which the sound of the radio can afford him. In addition, through television one is able to experience by proxy an event while it is taking place, both auditorially and visually. Thus in the comfort of his home, with conveniences he could not enjoy at the scene, one is able to be at the coliseum or public square, as with his ancient counterparts, and share in virtually everything which the man on the spot can experience. And while he may miss something of the added electricity of body power existing in the "touchable" group, he nevertheless has added advantages. These are special views, both close-ups and from various angles, and the additional pleasure of slow motion and instant replay. What is more, he is able to relive this experience the next day through newspaper reports and pictures and a week later through periodical editorializing, this time with colored pictures. Later, through the movie (on television or at a theater), he is able to relive the whole experience—this time "in living color."

Extremely significant for our understanding of mass man in the modern megalopolis is the recognition that he is able to experience (indeed often does experience) most if not all of the institutions of mass media represented by the great urban waves and the great communication revolutions of history, and is able to do this simultaneously or within a span of a few days.

Implication: The Impact-Penetration Principle

It should be very obvious at this point that man residing within a mass society has always lived in two worlds: (1) the private world of personal and primary group relations, and (2) the public world of mass relations. In order to communicate with man in the massive urban context, therefore, communication must be directed both to the level of the massive structures to which he relates and at the level of the primary group relationships of which he is a part. Mass communication is needed for impact, and personal communication is needed for penetration. These are complementary, however, and they are needed in balance for the most effective communication of the gospel in an urban society. Out of this reality comes the evangelistic principle of impact-penetration balance in communication which has fundamental implications for church growth in an urban world.

Notes

[1] Louis Wirth, "Urbanism as a Way of Life," *The American Journal of Sociology,* July, 1938, pp. 10–18.

[2] *The Sociology of Georg Simmel,* trans. by Kurt Wolff (Glencoe: The Free Press, 1950), pp. 409–17.

[3] William E. Cole, "Communications in Urban Life," *Urban Sociology* (Boston: Houghton Mufflin Co., 1958), pp. 353–63.

PART II

History: How Churches *Have* Grown

3 The Urban First Century

One of the clearest pictures in the New Testament is that, despite numerous references to pastoral scenes, the major events of the unfolding gospel story transpired in the city. The Christian church emerged in the social context of the urban first century. The apostolic church was an urban church.

The Unfolding Drama of Church Growth

Jesus and the City
Jesus was born in the city of Bethlehem, grew up in the city of Nazareth, and was crucified and resurrected in the city of Jerusalem. It is true that Bethlehem and Nazareth in Jesus' day were small towns by modern comparisons. Yet compared to the simple Bedouin culture of the times, they reflected a considerable sophistication. Jerusalem was an awesome urban center compared to the general social context of the day.

Jesus loved the city and wept over it: "O Jerusalem, Jerusalem, killing the prophets and stoning those who are sent to you! How often would I have gathered your children together as a hen gathers her brood under her wings, and you would not!" (Matt. 23:37).[1] The major thrust of our Lord's ministry was in the population centers of his day: "And Jesus went about all the cities and villages, teaching in their synagogues and preaching the gospel of the Kingdom, and healing every disease and every infirmity. When he saw the crowds, he had compassion for them" (Matt. 9:35–36).

As a fitting climax to his earthly ministry, Jesus commanded his disciples to tarry in the city of Jerusalem until they were endued with power from on high (Luke 24:49). They were admonished to tarry, not in some rural haven, not in some desert cave, but in the city of Jerusalem—where he had been crucified, where a hostile urban establishment prevailed, where the problems were, where the action was, where the influence was.

Jerusalem: The Base and the Beginning

It is significant that the church had its beginning in Jerusalem (of course, the church existed in embryonic form earlier). As an urban movement, it was indigenous to its context. From the beginning it assumed the complexion of an urban institution. The evangelism of the early church took on a massive character in keeping with the institution of the mass public meeting typical of the first great urban wave. Mass evangelism grew out of indigenous mass phenomena related to the events inherent in the socioreligious culture of the day, such as the celebration of the Feast of Pentecost where 3,000 people were converted and added to the young church (Acts 2). This mass evangelism continued and became an integral feature of the line of communication established by the early Christian community with its urban setting. Both in the temple and in the public plazas, the church proclaimed its message in harmony with the urban style of the mass public meeting.

In keeping with normative urban patterns, however, not all communication was mass communication. Personal communication was vital, and this was achieved on a one-to-one basis and especially through small groups in the homes. "And every day in the temple and at home they did not cease teaching and preaching Jesus as the Christ" (Acts 5:42). This reveals not only the content of their message, it reveals as well the style of their evangelism. There was the impact of mass evangelism through the temple and open plaza public gatherings and the penetration of personal evangelism through personal encounter and small group meetings in the homes.

This balance in personal and mass communication in the apostolic church is well illustrated from Acts 3. The apostles Peter and John were able to communicate and minister personally to the lame man at the Temple gate called "Beautiful." Later through the excitement caused by the healing of the lame man, Peter stood on the portico of Solomon and proclaimed the Christian message to the urban masses which gathered.

Another urban characteristic which the early church exhibited was mobility. The church, like its urban context, was not static. Through a vital flexibility, it was able to relate to its dynamic urban context. Thus it moved with its message and its ministry to the temple, to the open plazas, to the homes, to the market-places.

Mass Evangelism in the City of Samaria

The fires of mass evangelism which began in Jerusalem spread to Samaria. Philip, a preaching deacon, was the instrument in that extension of Christian influence. In Samaria, "the multitudes with one accord gave heed to what was said by Philip" (Acts 8:6). So great was the response that the apostles at Jerusalem, hearing the good report, sent Peter and John to Samaria to develop the new Christian community there (Acts 8:14).

The Antiochian Model: the Impact Principle

The second Christian center after Jerusalem was Antioch, a chief city of Syria. Out of the deep worshipful atmosphere of this church came the spiritual thrust which initiated the Christian missionary enterprise (Acts 13:1–4). From this urban congregation, the apostle Paul launched his great missionary career which eventuated in the planting of churches in the major urban centers of the Mediterranean world. The first mention of this church focused upon its deep inward life of worship and fellowship, and the impact of that spiritual vitality had such profound implications for the faith that it set the course for the young Christian movement for generations to come.

The Urban Strategy of Paul

The apostle Paul employed a decisive urban strategy in his evangelistic ministry. He did not work from a planned itinerary, apparently, but when a territory opened to him, he sought to reach it from the vantage point of the most strategic population center of the area. The cities which figured prominently in Paul's ministry were centers of administration, centers of Greek culture, centers of Jewish influence, and centers of commerce and trade. To trace Paul's missionary journeys is to discover a veritable catalog of cities. His pattern of ministry was to enter a city, preach and minister, gather converts, form a church with its own indigenous leaders, and move on. He kept in touch with these often fledgling congregations through letters. Where possible, he visited them, usually trying to backtrack after an extended missionary tour. In some cases he was able to send others to work with them, but in most cases the churches depended upon their own converted community leaders for spiritual guidance.

Paul's self-image was that of an apostle and minister, but the supreme direction of that apostleship and ministry was as a church planter. He was an evangelist, to be sure, but the fruit of his evangelistic ministry was churches. Roland Allen in his classic study, *Missionary Methods: Saint Paul's or Ours,* comments upon this remarkable work of Paul:

In little more than ten years Saint Paul established the church in four provinces of the Empire, Galatia, Macedonia, Achaia and Asia. Before A.D. 47 there were no churches in these provinces; in A.D. 57 Saint Paul could speak as if the work there was done, and could plan extensive tours into the far west without anxiety lest the churches which he had founded might perish in his absence for want of his guidance or support.

The work of the apostle during these ten years can therefore be treated as a unit. Whatever assistance he may have received from the preaching of others, it is unquestioned that the establishment of the Churches in these provinces was really his work. In the pages of the New Testament he, and he alone, stands forth as their founder. And the work which he did was really a completed work. So far as the foundation of the Churches is concerned, it is perfectly clear that the writer of Acts intends to represent Saint Paul's work as complete. The Churches were really established. Whatever disasters fell upon them in later years, whatever failure there was, whatever ruin, that failure was not due to any insufficiency or lack of care or completeness in the Apostle's teaching or organization. When he left them he left them because his work was fully accomplished.

This is truly an astonishing fact. That churches should be founded so rapidly, so securely, seems to us today, accustomed to the difficulties, the uncertainties, the failures, the disastrous lapses of our own missionary work, almost incredible. Many missionaries in later days have received a larger number of converts than Saint Paul; many have preached over a wider area than he; but none have so established churches.[2]

[The apostle Paul not only was clearly conscious of his intention to establish the Christian witness in significant urban centers, he understood well that urban context.] The ancient institution of the mass public meeting had one of its most sophisticated expressions in Athens. And Paul well illustrated its use. After he was driven from Thessalonica and Berea, he took refuge in Athens. However, the very sight of the idolatry of the city deeply offended his Judeo-Christian sensitivities, and he went to the synagogue and marketplaces daily to discuss the matter with the Jews and proselytes (God-fearing Gentiles). Here he also encountered some Epicurean and Stoic philosophers. Because he was dealing with matters that interested them, he was invited to the Areopagus (Ares Hill or Mars' Hill). Athens was a city of learning and therefore attracted philosophers and miscellaneous inquirers and seekers. Therefore, one form the ancient institution of the mass public meeting took in Athens was a special place designated as an open forum for anyone who had something of an idealogical nature to share (it was a rock formation creating a natural stage). This was as much an institution of ancient Athens as the theater or marketplace. And like them, it was a significant instrument of mass communication. This illustrates the extent of the urbanization which both influenced and was influenced by the apostle. The impact Paul was able to make on Athens was not felt immediately, but in time it proved to be one of considerable import.

The Ephesian Model: The Penetration Principle

The master model of Paul's strategy is Ephesus. [Here he was not only successful in starting a church, he was able also to establish it as a center from which the gospel successfully penetrated the whole of Asia Minor. As in the past, Paul made an effort in Ephesus to use the synagogue as an instrument of communication. He was successful for three months. His audience (perhaps the larger audience in and around the synagogue) is referred to by Luke as being "the multitude." Soon, however, Paul was forced out of the synagogue, and he then used the Hall of Tyrannus from which he preached for two years. Already there were "disciples" whom he took with him from the synagogue to the school of Tyrannus. Therefore the nucleus of the Ephesian church had already been established. Acts 19 records that Paul had a strong healing as well as preaching ministry in Ephesus.

The impact of Paul's ministry in Ephesus itself was phenomenal. Lives were deeply affected. For example, those who had engaged in magic brought their books to be burned, the value of which has been estimated to be the equivalent of a day's wages for 50,000 people. Luke says, "Fear fell upon them all; and the name of the Lord Jesus was extolled" (v. 17). A result of this was that "the Word of the Lord grew and prevailed mightily" (v. 20).

In addition to the impact upon Ephesus itself by the mass public meetings conducted by Paul, the Ephesian church became a significant center whose influence was felt over all Asia Minor. We do not have the specifics of the Pauline strategy by which this was accomplished, but the book of Acts makes it clear that "all the residents of Asia heard the Word of the Lord, both Jews and Greeks" (v. 10). We are not certain how many churches were started during this period (Luke speaks simply of "all hearing the Word"). We do know that there were a number of congregations in strategic places over Asia Minor soon after this period. One indication of this is the seven churches of Asia referred to in Revelation 2 and 3.

The Reach for Rome—the Reach for the World

The Old Testament develops a sophisticated ideology around the theme of the city, as we shall see later. However, the New Testament presents a different kind of urban symbolism. It is true that Jesus condemned such cities as Capernaum, Tyre, and

Sidon in much the same way the prophets had condemned such cities as Nineveh, Babylon, Samaria, and even Jerusalem. However, the gospel brought a new dimension to the meaning of the city. While retaining the ancient mystique of Jerusalem and establishing the new Jerusalem as the ultimate goal of the spiritual pilgrimage, the early church at the same time developed a much more pragmatic view of the city.

Paul came to see the city not in terms of good and evil to be praised or to be blamed in the tradition of early biblical writers. He saw the city rather as the theater of mission—not simply the context in which evangelism and ministry take place, but also a strategic point of influence and therefore the base of operation for the worldwide expansion of the gospel. Therefore, Rome as the ultimate earthly city, takes on a powerful symbolic meaning in relationship to God's ultimate purpose in the gospel. "All roads lead to Rome," goes the old saying, and it therefore follows that out from Rome roads lead to the ends of the earth. Paul may very well have been thinking that if the gospel could be soundly planted in the imperial capital of the world, it would have the best possible opportunity to spread to the rest of the earth. Therefore with deep thought and emotion he wrote to the Roman Christians: "So I am eager to preach the gospel to you also who are in Rome. For I am not ashamed of the gospel: it is the power of God for salvation to everyone who has faith" (Rom. 1:15–16).

How the Churches Grew

The New Testament makes it quite clear that churches grew phenomenally in the apostolic period. How did the churches grow? Why did they grow? What contributed to their growth? Equally important: How can we learn from this pattern of urban church growth?

The Spiritual Base

Theology always precedes methodology. The method can only grow out of the message. The New Testament makes this clear. The early church grew because it had the spiritual resources for growth. This is the first principle of church growth, without which all other principles are in vain. First, there was the reassuring presence of the risen Lord himself. Then there was the commission, the clear call to mission. Then came the Spirit's anointing and the power for change which he released. Finally, there was the worshiping fellowship. Out of these resources came the impetus for mission. "For we cannot but speak of what we have seen and heard" (Acts 4:20). It was from this inward spiritual strength that the Jerusalem church broke forth on mission with such evangelistic power. It was from this same inward power that the Antioch church caught the Spirit's vision and sent forth those first missionaries, Paul and Barnabas, changing the face of the earth for all time. It was with this same inward certainty—not always dramatic—sometimes against all but overwhelming odds—that Paul laid that foundation of the Christian congregations which gave the Christian movement its initial base for its first extensive thrust into the world.

The Means of Growth

Teaching and preaching and healing was the profoundly simple method of Jesus in his urban evangelism. The apostolic community in Jerusalem continued that same method. Philip and Paul followed the same tradition. There were no gimmicks. There was no need for them. The gospel compelled preaching, the message compelled teaching, and the love of God compelled healing.

It is interesting that Paul's preoccupation was with preaching, teaching, and reaching out in a healing ministry. He never seemed aware of a church planting strategy as such. The message and the ministry produced the converts and the converts produced the congregation. It followed as light follows the sun.

Indigenous to the Urban Context

Two complementary elements are necessary for any effective communication: a relevant message and an authentic recipient. We can assume that the gospel message is relevant, that it is universal, able to speak authentically both to the human situation in general and to any specific human need in particular.

For the gospel to have an authentic recipient, it must be addressed to the recipient in the way he or she is able to receive communication. This is the first principle of indigenity. The gospel therefore must be communicated to masses or individuals through the channels of the specific culture to which these masses and individuals belong. The church is God's instrument through which his message is communicated. Therefore, the church must be indigenous to its cultural context if it is to serve effectively as God's instrument. We have observed earlier how the early church from the start was indigenous to its context. It was able therefore to establish meaningful communication with its urban constituency. Also the early church, indigenous to its context, was able to move with the movement of its social context. As a mobile institution, its structures were flexible and therefore adaptable to the ever-changing demands of the urban scene.

Scholars have been careful to point out the readiness of the times for the coming of the Messiah and the founding and the growth of the church. What is often overlooked, however, is that much of that "fullness of time" phenomena was in practical reality the result of an urban technology. Cities emerged in history with the development of tools, and cities have increased in complexity with the improvement of tools and technical methods.

The early church related to the technology of its time. For example, the Roman roads were part of the new technology. The Romans, through their technological expertise, created a network of roads unknown to man before that time. It was precisely along those travel arteries that the gospel first moved and multiplied. Moreover it was in the cities created by the technologies of that time that the gospel was first planted and the Christian movement began.

The development of a sophisticated language which became the trade language and the literary medium of the time (the Greek language), making all subcultural groups a part of one profound network of communication, was another aspect of the technology of the first century cities. The gospel was communicated through this language both by spoken and by written word. We, as our first century counterparts, must move with the technology of our times, employing such technology both as the medium of our message and the tool of our evangelistic methodology. Thus in an uncanny and almost incredible way, the New Testament furnishes us raw material out of which to understand our evangelistic task today. It prepares us with the perfect ideology out of which to forge an adequate theology of communication for the mass cultures of our modern urban world.

Kinds of Growth

The book of Acts gives considerable attention to the quantitative or numerical growth of the church during the apostolic period. The early Christian community began with about 120 persons (1:15), and on the day of Pentecost about 3,000 souls were added to that small company (2:41). There were increases from day to day according to Acts 2:47. Very early the number of disciples amounted to some 5,000 men, not counting the women (4:4). According to Acts 5:14 multitudes of men and women continued to be added to the community of faith. According to Acts 6:1,7 the number of disciples "multiplied greatly," and "many of the priests were obedient to the faith." Despite the persecution that came which scattered the church except for the apostles, the church contined to grow (9:31; 12:24). According to Acts 21:20 Paul learned during a visit to Jerusalem that "many thousands" of Jews had become Christians. Multitudes responded to Philip's ministry in Samaria (Acts 8), and Acts 9:35 says, "All the residents of Lydda and Sharon . . . turned to the Lord." It is reported in Acts 9:42 that "many believed in the Lord" in the significant port city of Joppa.

As the Christian movement spread further north, "a great number that believed turned to the Lord" in Antioch of Syria (11:21). On Paul's first missionary journey, Acts records that "the Word of the Lord spread throughout all the region" of Antioch of Pisidia (13:49). Acts 14:1 records that in Iconium "a great company be-

lieved, both of Jews and of Greeks." On his next missionary journey, Paul accompanied by Silas, visited many of the churches
he had founded earlier. As a result "the churches were strengthened in the faith, and they increased in number daily" (16:5).

As Paul moved westward across the Aegean he found great
response in the cities of Macedonia. In Thessalonica "a great
many of devout Greeks and not a few of the leading women"
as well as some Jews were converted (17:4). In Berea, many believed, including "not a few Greek women of high standing as
well as men" (v. 12). In Athens the response to Paul's message
was not impressive except with regard to the quality of the few
converts (v. 34). However, a little later "many of the Corinthians"
as well as persons of high repute such as Crispus, the ruler of
the synagogue, and his household were baptized (18:8). Extensive
reference has already been made to the incredible growth of the
work in Asia Minor during Paul's stay at the strategic city of
Ephesus.

[In addition to the careful reporting of numerical growth, Luke
seems to be equally concerned to list with precision the spread
of the faith in its geographical extension.] Jerusalem was strategic.
From Jerusalem the gospel spread throughout Judea and into
Galilee and Samaria. Soon the gospel spread to Antioch of Syria.
From here the missionary journeys of Paul carried the gospel
westward through Asia Minor and then to strategic urban centers
in what is presently Greece. Paul's passion for Rome is explained
in part by his desire to extend the geographical boundaries of
the Christian witness. To the end of this incredible missionary
career, he was dreaming of extending further the geographical
influence of the Christian message.

[There was also an emphasis upon qualitative growth.] The account of the quality of spiritual life in the Jerusalem and Antioch
churches is one of the most inspiring pictures of the entire chronicle of the apostolic church. The book of Acts is careful to point
out that the church was "built up" as well as "multiplied" (9:31);
that it was strengthened in the faith as well as "increased in num-

bers" (16:5). It was not simply the community of faith which increased but the Word of the Lord "grew and multiplied" (12:24) and "prevailed mightily" (19:20).

Structure of the Church

We shall deal in a later section with the theological issues of the urban church, but it should be mentioned at this stage that the apostolic church was a community of faith. It was in no sense a building, as the church has come in one sense to be today. It did have structure, however, and in the New Testament era, it was a clearly definable institution. Its institutionalized manifestations were essentially two-fold: as gathered in community for worship and fellowship, and as dispersed on mission for evangelism and ministry. The church is described in both of these functions in the New Testament. These functions were harmonious, however, and seemed to exist in a kind of spiritual rhythm. They complemented each other and were never separated in the minds of the early believers or the New Testament authors.

The gathered church had essentially two structured forms: the more mass-type meeting and the more personalized small-type group. Mass meetings at certain times were held in public places, especially evangelistic type situations. At first the Jerusalem church used the Temple for its mass-type meetings. Later Paul used the synagogue, marketplaces, and the open air for such meetings. However, later for an enclosed meeting place, the more secularized school of Tyrannus seemed to serve Paul and the Ephesian congregation better. It did not occur to Paul, apparently, to erect his own building. As a tentmaker, he might very well have made a large tent to house the Ephesian congregation and his base of missionary outreach. There seems to be evident theological reasons for avoiding this. The church was in no sense to be identified with a place or to become localized in that sense. It was neither tabernacle nor temple in the Old Testament sense. It was the people of God.

Nevertheless Paul definitely felt the need of a meeting place for the mass-type meetings of the Ephesian church. The apparently large facility of the hall of Tyrannus seemed to be primarily an evangelistic and missionary center, the base for the massive and penetrative thrust into Asia Minor.

The more personalized small group meetings were held in homes. In fact it was the home more than anything else that housed the New Testament congregations. There is an obvious affinity between the church and the home in the New Testament theology. As long as the early Christians were permitted in the temples and synagogues, they met there on various occasions. However, the homes seemed more conducive to the full expression of the life of the Christian community. Though both the Temple and the home provided the context for preaching and teaching Jesus Christ daily (Acts 5:42), the church in its more sustained life of fellowship met in the homes. When Saul the persecutor wanted to find Christians in numbers, he went neither to the Temple nor to the synagogues—he went to the homes. "But Saul laid waste the church, and entering house after house, he dragged off men and women and committed them to prison" (8:3).

From the earliest pages of Acts, the Spirit of God seems to select the home as the scene for the deepest developments in the life of the church. When on the day of Pentecost the Spirit of God visited the people of God as a rushing mighty wind, his presence "filled all the *house* where they were sitting" (2:2). Under the impetus of the Spirit's visitation, day by day they broke bread "in their *homes*" (v. 46). "Every day . . . at *home*" they taught and preached Jesus Christ (5:42). It was in the *house* of Cornelius, the Italian, that Peter visited and the Holy Spirit fell, in one of the most significant movements of the gospel in the apostolic period (Acts 10). After the Philippian jailer received the message of Paul and Silas, he brought them "into his *house,* and set food before them; and he rejoiced with all his household that he believed in God" (16:34). Moreover, before Paul and Silas left Philippi, they visited the home of Lydia and exhorted the brethren before they departed (v. 40). When Paul admonished Timothy concerning how to behave in "the household of God, which is the church of the living God, the pillar and bulwark of the truth" (1 Tim.

3:15), he was not referring to a church building, but rather to the assembled family of God.

The only churches of the New Testament which are listed with a specific location beyond a general community geographical designation are identified with certain homes. There are at least three of these mentioned in the New Testament. There was a church in the house of Prisca and Aquila. In writing to the Roman Christians, Paul sent special greetings to Prisca and Aquila and to "the church in their house" (Rom. 16:3–5). Moreover, Paul writing from Rome to the Corinthian church, conveyed special greetings from Prisca and Aquila along "with the church in their house" (1 Cor. 16:19). There was a church in the house of Nympha. In writing to the Colossian Christians, Paul sent salutations to the Laodicean Christians and to Nympha and to "the church in her house" (Col. 4:15). There was a church in the house of Philemon. In writing to Philemon on behalf of Onesimus, Paul addressed himself to others besides Philemon and to the church in Philemon's house— "to Philemon, our beloved fellow worker, and Apphia our sister and Archippus our fellow-soldier, and the church in your house" (Philem. 1–2).

It appears that the homes were the scene of church worship, fellowship, and some teaching and evangelism. The rented halls seemed to have been primarily for preaching and teaching the gospel. We therefore observe that the early church assumed two forms in keeping with the norms of communication in the urban context: the mass type meeting for evangelistic impact and the small group meeting primarily in the homes for nurture and fellowship.

It is significant to note that the urban strategy employed by Paul had a profound influence on the pattern of establishing cities not simply as gospel strongholds but as bases for missionary outreach. The patterns of church growth in the generations that followed are witness to this, as new urban centers within and without the Mediterranean sphere emerged as evangelistic and missionary strongholds. Antioch of Syria and Ephesus continued for sometime beyond the New Testament period as just such centers. Rome was the third great Christian urban center after Jerusalem and Antioch. After the New Testament era there developed a long list of significant urban centers which continued this vital function of evangelistic and missionary strongholds. Some began but were not strong in the apostolic period. Others appeared after the account in Acts. The list is impressive: Corinth, Thessalonica, Caesarea of Cappadocia, Alexandria, Damascus, Edessa, Hippo Regius, Constantinople, Tours, Milan, Lyons. Although these cities possessed varing degrees of importance, they were all significant in the growth of the church in the early centuries after the close of the apostolic era.

Notes

[1] All Scripture quotations are from the Revised Standard Version of the Bible, copyright 1946, 1952 ©, 1971, 1973.

[2] Roland Allen, *Missionary Methods: Saint Paul's or Ours* (Chicago: Moody Press, 1959), pp. 3–4.

4 The Recent Urban Past

Because most of the patterns of modern urban church life have their roots in the recent urban past, we shall not attempt to survey urban church growth prior to that. The apostolic church did not produce complex church congregational types. The church was young and the time span in the New Testament period was quite brief. Moreover, the cities of the first century, although complex by the general standards of the age, did not have the complex form and life typical of the modern city. Only the last two centuries, with their great urban development and evangelical church growth, have produced the variety of Christian congregational types we know today. Recent urbanization and the complex urban expressions which they have spawned is as much responsible for this variety as the variedness of Protestantism itself. This is well illustrated by the fact that given enough time each denomination will develop essentially all of the various geographic types of urban congregations.

Growth by Congregational Types

The Renaissance era produced two institutions which have strongly influenced the style of modern urban congregational life: the cathedral and the village church. The Reformation and the Industrial Revolution added a third influence: the ideological congregation. These were the congregations—first the Reformed and later the Baptists, Methodists, and others—which were created out of the emerging middle class with its new ideological awareness. This phenomenon was not an expression of either urban form or life as such. It was urban in the ultimate sense, however, in that the city has always been the scene of change. Moreover, it is not an accidental scene, for the city's very nature provides the ingredients and dynamics not simply necessary for but conducive to change. Every Christian congregation in the city can be understood in part on the basis of these influences. It is therefore important to understand these roots and their influence on the style of Christian congregations in modern urban society.

The reason it is important to study church congregational types is the simple fact that the church grows by a proliferation of distinct congregational types. What is more, these churches can be classified and explained essentially on the basis of their roots and their style.

Congregational Classifications

A number of helpful classifications of both general and urban congregations have been offered in studies over the last few decades. Although these are recent studies, most of them reflect the late metropolitan scene. That is, they deal with the essential congregational types typical of the period ending roughly around mid-century. Some do not reflect the more radical and recent developments of the sixties and seventies.

An International Typology

C. Peter Wagner classifies city churches on the basis of current international models.[1] He sees five essential types: the cathedral, the storefront, the outer city or suburban church, the house church, the ethnic church. He divides the cathedral into two subclasses. The "traditional" is the classical Catholic, Anglican, or Reformed cathedral and perhaps in some cases "Old First." The "newer" would be the congregational types which others would classify as the downtown church, the uptown church, the people's church, or the large residential church of older and newer Protestant denominations. Wagner's treatment of other types is rather typical, but it is striking that he does not mention the most common city church. This is the small and medium-size residential congregation or small and medium-size congregation which may not be a neighborhood church in the traditional sense but at the same time is not a cathedral, a storefront, a suburban church, a house church, or an ethnic church. Whether they are typically a neighborhood type or are more regional in style, whether they are stable or are threatened by transition, these small and medium size congregations constitute the majority of the city churches the world over. Perhaps Wagner intends to include at least some of these in the outer city or suburban church. However, they are primarily inner city or central city churches, certainly not suburban churches in the usual meaning of the term. Despite this limitation, this classification is very helpful in illustrating the international character of urban church congregational life.

A Japanese Typology

Robert Lee's study of the church in Japan provides a helpful classification of five urban congregational types.[2] He gives profiles of five urban congregations: "Inner City Church," which is the identifying church; "Workingman's Church," which is a church of prayerful concern; "Downtown Church," which is the open church, "Uptown Church," which is the church of solemn worship; "Suburban Church," which is a church of town and gown. This type of study with its careful classification of style is especially helpful at the point of illustrating the strong similarity between the urban congregation of the East and that of the West, illustrating quite clearly the influence of Western models upon Eastern congregational types. It is also valuable in that it reflects the unique Japanese urban scene as well as universal patterns which are to be found among urban churches the world over.

A North American Typology

The Methodist denomination has done a number of helpful studies on the urban church in the United States in which the classification of churches has proved to be integral to its investigation. These studies, which are based upon various congregational types and their urban environments, have been significant because they apply to urban church life of most denominations. The parallels between these Methodist congregational types and their histories and those of Baptists are for all practical purposes exact. A special series of three studies was published in 1958.[3] They classify urban congregations as follows: the downtown church, the inner city church, the residential church. The inner city church is subdivided into the old high status church, the small neighborhood church, the language or ethnic church, and the Negro church. This classification reflects essentially the types of urban congregations which were apparent at the close of the metropolitan era.

A General North American Classification

Because North America has developed the most varied types of urban churches and because of the international influence of these models and their styles, an appreciation of these types and the influences that have both shaped and threatened them is invaluable for an understanding of the beginning, growth, decline, and demise of urban churches.

The Cathedral

The cathedral reached a high stage of development during the Renaissance and has continued into modern times as one of the most urban of all church institutions. It especially flourished during the era of the metropolis, reaching its greatest heights as a religious center in the heart of the city. The Anglican and Reformed types, of course, have been based upon the Catholic model. The cathedral traditionally has been located in the central, usually downtown, area of the city and has been metropolitan in its outreach. Its constituency has been citywide, and it has traditionally related to a wide variety of urban inhabitants. At the same time it has always claimed the most influential church people in the city. As the seat of the diocese or the headquarters of the denomination, its influence has been as impressive as its architecture has been imposing. It has long been an essential feature both of the landscape and the sociology of the city. The symbolism of its visibility on the central city scene has always been marked, whether or not it has been a state church.

Cathedrals in their grandest form, of course, are located in

Europe. However, they are to be found the world over, not simply in places where Christianity has been the dominant faith. It is difficult to measure the congregational strength of the cathedral because it is more than a congregation. Even when its constituency begins to fail, it has the resources of the state, the diocese, or denomination upon which to rely. Because it has had the best of leadership and because it often has special services and regional meetings, its audience does not always reflect the true strength of the congregational life resident within the cathedral facility.

Downtown "Old First"

The first urban church in areas where the Free Church traditions prevail was the town church. As the town developed into the small city, residential churches sprang up and the original town church came in time to be known as the downtown church. It usually took the name "First" at this time, if it had not done so earlier. The downtown church developed into the classic model of "Old First." It became the cathedral of "Free Church tradition." A metropolitan church serving the whole city, it developed into a large prestigious congregation of both professional and working-class people. Traditionally it has been the home church of the city's leading citizens. It has tended to reflect the heterogeneity of the city as a whole and thus has developed a strictly urban style from its identity to its ministry. In its service to the city, it has tended to be flexible and mobile reflecting the mood and movement of its urban environment. It has been a strong supporter both financially and morally of the denomination, with the pastor often being a leader in denominational life. It has served as the unofficial voice of the denomination in the city, and in some cases it actually houses the local denominational headquarters. The church plant usually has been an imposing and excellent facility, massive and often cathedral-like. It has served as a profound religious symbol in the city, both of its denomination's presence in the city and of faith in general among other institutions in central city life. In cities strongly dominated by a given Free Church tradition where there has been no cathedral, it has been socially and religiously for all practical purposes a cathedral.

Old First has been traditionally a large congregation with a multiple staff. In the metropolitan era it represented by far the largest churches in the country. It has had a strong pulpit ministry, an active music program, a strong religious education program and especially effective ministries to children and youth. It has had a special appeal to downtown minded people, newcomers to the city, singles, and the elderly. It has long been characterized by strong congregational leadership and a devotedly loyal, but widely scattered, membership.

During this period downtown churches in the older cities of the north and eastern United States have tended to be affected by the changes that were beginning to take shape in the urban centers even before World War II.

The Uptown Church

As the cities grew, and consequently the city churches in the era of the metropolis, a number of semidowntown congregations emerged. From the beginning some of these were not strictly residential churches. In most larger cities a few of these have emerged as large congregations with a wide range of appeal to metropolitan residents. During the latter part of the last century, and especially the early part of this century, many of these large congregations assumed a completion and role comparable to the downtown Old First church. However, strictly speaking this congregation may better be called the uptown church because usually it has been located more in the direction of a major secondary business district than in the central business district. It has been, however, more of a business district than a residential church. It is distinct from the downtown Old First in a number of ways. It was not the first congregation of its denomination in the city. It usually has been formed out of the downtown church, either as a split or as a mission. To some degree it has been a residential church, though essentially it has been metropolitan in its identity and outreach.

The uptown church may go by the name "Second" since in

many cases it was the second church of its denomination to be started in the city. Earlier in its history it may have served a distinct residential area, especially before it grew to the size where it was able to take on a metropolitan character. Sometimes this congregation has taken the name "Metropolitan," or it may have taken the name of an important street such as Broadway.

Though the uptown church is distinct from the downtown church, it does have some of the features of downtown Old First. Like Old First it has been a large church with a multiple staff and an impressive facility. It has had in its membership some of the most prominent people in the city. In some cases it has tended to be a more professional type church than First Church. Though it has been metropolitan in its appeal, it has not been normally as metropolitan as the downtown church. It has tended to draw principally from the nearest stable and elite communities whereas Old First draws more generally from the entire city. Traditionally, it has been nearer the better part of the town economically. It has a status comparable to Old First and in some cases has even developed to be a more prestigious church than the downtown church. In fact this congregational type has sometimes been called "the old high status church." Even though it is usually one of the city's older churches and one with a rich tradition, it is younger than Old First and is usually composed of younger people. It tends to be, as a general rule, more progressive. In some cases the uptown church, because it had tended to be more progressive and has retained some semblance of a parish, has stood the test of change better than Old First.

The People's Church

Another distinctive congregational type which emerged during the metropolitan era is the people's church. It has been a kind of poor man's downtown or uptown church. It is not a residential church but is metropolitan in character, drawing its members from the city at large. Traditionally, it has been composed predominantly of lower middle-class people. A large country church in the city, it is the common man's cathedral. Even though this type congregation usually has been very large with a leading pulpit ministry, it has not been in the usual sense a status church. Usually it has been a congregation of warm fellowship and a decidedly free spirit in its services. It has been very conservative theologically and very aggressive evangelistically. In some cases it has developed professional and even wealthy people.

As a rule these people tend to have a rural background and a strong folk orientation. These congregations have usually taken such names as Tabernacle or Temple though it is not uncommon for them to have such typical church names as Calvary. The second generation in this congregation may tend to turn it into more of an uptown type church, depending upon the circumstances, especially if there is a more socially favorable relocation. Ordinarily this church had been located on or near a thoroughfare in an economically less desirable area of the city, usually in the direction of the industrial complex of the metropolis.

Because the people's church has not had the reserve of wealth, education, prestige, and tradition typical of the downtown and uptown church, it has tended to be more affected by change. This type congregation is capable of great and rapid decline in the face of change. It usually suffers greatly or dies unless it produces a second generation of greater affluence or makes a shift in emphasis or makes a move to a more favorable location. In cases where the churches have had unusually strong leadership, it has not only resisted urban social change but has emerged to be in some cases phenomenal in size.

The University Church

Another congregational type which emerged in the era of the metropolis is the university church. As the name implies, this is a congregation which has traditionally served the university community, though its ministry has not necessarily been limited to that community. It is fairly common in relatively small cities for the downtown or uptown church or even the large neighborhood church to function also as a university church. This has been true in cases where the university community has been located in the uptown area or in a residential area served by a large congregation. In most large cities, however, the university church has been a distinct congregation from the uptown church or the large residential church. How this congregation has fared in the changes which were beginning to take place even before World War II in the older Northern and Eastern cities of the United States has depended to a larger degree upon how stable the community has been in which it was located. If the church has been located in an inner city community near the university or college, often the university people tend to live in the suburbs, and the congregation has consequently suffered. If the congregation and the university have been in a stable neighborhood, then the university people tend to live in the university community, and the congregation reaps the benefits.

The Large Neighborhood Church

A distinct type of city church which emerged during this era is the large neighborhood or residential church. This church has usually been located in a stable neighborhood. It has usually had a long history compared to most central city neighborhood churches. Because it has been large, it has functioned in part as a metropolitan church and may blend in type with the uptown church. In smaller cities these two tend to be one and the same in distinction from the Old First and other city congregations. This congregation like the downtown and uptown church, has had a strong pulpit ministry, a multiple staff, an imposing facility, and an outstanding program. However, it has been basically a residential church. It may have taken the traditional name such as Calvary or Immanuel, or it may have taken the name of its community such as Highland Park, especially since its community has tended in most cases to be one of the better neighborhoods in the city. Because it has been an older church with some tradition, because it has been large, and because it has usually been favorably located in the city, it has tended to stand the test of change better than the smaller, younger, or less favorably situated neighborhood churches.

The Medium-sized Neighborhood Church

Another type of congregation prominent in the metropolitan era has been the medium-sized neighborhood or residential church. This has been the most common congregational type in the city. Traditionally it has served a distinct community, and it usually has taken the name of that community, though it often has taken such common congregational names as Calvary, Grace, or Bethany. How this church fares in the urban setting usually has depended upon the stability of the community or how well the church has been able to change to meet the new needs of the changing community in which it exists.

The Small Neighborhood Church

In every city there have always been a number of small neighborhood churches that never seem to be able to spark much growth. However, these churches have held on decades on end and sometimes for generations while stronger churches decline and die around them. These churches, when linked with smaller churches in town, village, and country areas, constitute the largest single type of Christian congregation, namely, the small church.

The Storefront Church

A unique type of urban congregation which emerged as a separate congregational type the early part of this century is the storefront church. It has usually been a small group of people occupying a store building or old house. The people are usually poor with a fairly recent rural background. The congregation may be white, black, or ethnic. It may be denominational, but usually it has not been. These congregations have ranged from cults to Pentecostals to Baptists. To some the storefront has been a permanent home, to others simply a means to an end. The one characteristic feature of the storefront church has been its friendliness and warm fellowship. This is its supreme attraction.

The Black Church

As blacks moved from the rural South and migrated to the

cities, they carried with them their faith. Consequently, black churches have sprung up in great numbers all over the central cities of America. Some of the largest and most influential churches in America are black congregations. It was the metropolitan era that produced the black congregation as a distinct urban church type. Some of these black urban churches go back into the last century. Recently the Third Baptist Church of San Francisco, one of the most prestigious in the city, celebrated its 125th anniversary. The early part of this century witnessed a number of black churches in the central city emerging as leading congregations of that city. Many black congregations which began as humble storefront operations early in this century have in time come to be thriving churches with their own cathedral-like facilities. Most blacks in the United States have been of Methodist and Baptist background. Consequently, the Baptist and Methodist churches have tended to dominate the black communities. However, there are a growing number of Pentecostal congregations, and now many new cults and sect types have emerged. Another characteristic feature of the black church which has emerged primarily in this century has been the cult type headed by a strong charismatic leader.

The Ethnic Church

Another special type of congregation which took distinctive form during the metropolitan era is the ethnic-language church. In most cases these congregations began as language churches situated in a distinct ethnic community. When the need for the language no longer existed, these congregations have either continued essentially as ethnic churches or have reached out to serve the general community. In Detroit at one time there were four Romanian speaking churches. Now there is only one. One of these congregations made an especially meaningful transition into a nonethnic, English-speaking church. One of the dangers of this type congregation is that it tends to perpetuate the culture, and sometimes culture may become more significant in church life than faith itself. Many of these congregations have died because they refused to provide English services for their children and for nonethnic members of their neighborhood. In most cases these ethnic language congregations emerged in the social context of their ethnic subculture. As these communities began to change, however, some of these ethnic congregations were left as enclaves within a black ghetto, totally unrelated to their neighborhoods. In Detroit for example, Italian, Romanian, Czechoslovakian, and other ethnic-language churches had greatly declined by midcentury, and some of them had disbanded. In some cases it was the natural process of Americanization. This happened more with European congregations than with Asian, Latin American, native American, and Afro-American congregations. The current situation has greatly changed this picture, however, as we shall see later.

The Suburban Church

Even though it has been the urban revolution of post World War II which has produced the greatest suburban development in the history of the world, suburbs were beginning to develop rather significantly, especially in some of the older cities of the Western world, before this period. Consequently before World War II there was a growing community of suburban churches. Some of these churches were in semirural areas at the edge of cities. Some were in well-developed new communities beyond the city. Some were in areas far from the central city, but still within the city limits. This would especially be true of younger cities such as Houston. Some of these were villages and towns which had become large suburban communities because of their proximity to a large urban center. Because there was little growth and development during the era of the Depression and since the war years were not normative times, it took the immediate postwar period to provide the kind of suburban development which eventuated into the phenomenally growing suburban churches we know today.

How the Churches Grew

The metropolitan era provided the environment for the greatest growth of churches in the history of Christianity. Paradoxically, it also provided the environment for the changes which set the stage for conditions which have brought the greatest threat to churches since the rise of Islam. These reverse conditions were to appear later. Let us look now at the factors which contributed to growth in this period.

The Surge of Spiritual Vitality

There has never been a significant church growth movement without an antecedent spiritual awakening. Paralleling the secular developments centering in the Industrial Revolution and the vast urbanization which it produced, were spiritual movements such as the evangelical revivals and the modern mission movement. These movements had their roots in a deep piety in Europe and America especially noticeable in the Moravian and Wesleyan movements in Europe. After the turn of the century, Baptists and others such as the Pentecostal and Holiness groups caught this spirit and began to grow at a rapid pace.

Favorable Social Context

Like the urban first century, the social environment was conducive to church growth during the Industrial Revolution which set the basic pattern for recent urban developments. Because we have been so accustomed to thinking of urbanization in negative terms, seeing only its problems and taking for granted its blessings, we have not appreciated the positive environment it has provided for church growth. It was the urban Industrial Revolution which created a literate middle class which could take advantage of the emerging literature which, in turn, that miracle of urban technology, the printing press, was providing. The continuing improvement of this urban technology, especially in communication and transportation, brought unprecedented opportunities for the Christian faith in general and church growth in particular.

The Growing Complexity of Means

With the ever-expanding opportunities of an urban age came an ever expanding complexity in the urban style. As the Christian means of evangelism and ministry became more indigenous to a more complex urban style, the simple Christian methods of the past assumed a more elaborate expression.

Teaching developed into a number of institutional forms. The Sunday School movement and related developments brought an elaborate educational system to the churches. This was matched by the emergence of Christian colleges, Bible institutes, and theological seminaries. Education expanded to include special teaching conferences, seminars of almost endless number and style. Preaching became an institution with the urban pulpit playing a decisive role in shaping that style. The itinerate, the revivalist, and other preacher-types expanded this image.

The printed page, radio, and later television brought the preacher into the living rooms and marketplaces of urban man. Healing was expanded into clinics, hospitals, and sophisticated medical institutions which the Christian mission established the world over.

Paralleling these more complex institutions, mostly for the sick body, there grew up a whole world of person-centered and group-oriented therapists through whom the church ministered to the emotional and spiritual needs of urban man. The institution of "the teacher," the "chaplain," and numerous others were added to the "pastor" or "preacher," as the role of the minister became specialized to match the increasing specialization which is inherent in an expanding urbanism.

The Larger Christian Movement

A major contributing factor to the multiplication of Christian congregations during the metropolitan era was the growth of denominations. Out of the Reformation came the Anglicans and the mainline Protestant groups: Lutheran, Reformed, Presbyterian. In the early 1600s the Baptists and Congregationalists established themselves as a denomination. It was in the 1800s that the denominations took on the form which we know today. Indeed such major groups as Methodists and Disciples emerged during this period. Later the younger Holiness and Pentecostal groups emerged. The European state churches became denominations in North America. European and North American denominations had a profound influence on the rest of the world through their mission and educational programs. The urban based headquarters of mission and educational agencies became springboards for international church extension.

In addition to the denominations, ecumenical and interdenominational groups offered an additional base for the strengthening of the faith and consequently for the growth of churches. Lay institute movements further enhanced the outreach. Revivalism was a major factor in both the renewal and extension of the church. Evangelistic and missionary organizations were in the front of church extension around the world. Parachurch groups have been both complementary and competitive so far as the established church is concerned. New church groups have also been both complementary and competitive. Some church groups in this period grew at the expense of others, and many churches in this period were started through splits.

Urban Structure and Church Structure

We have observed that this period of urbanization brought a vast and extensive urban expression. It is significant that there developed through this period a church type to fit every phase of urban geography. It is further significant to note that the urban churches took on the same complexities of the urbanism which emerged in the society at large. Some congregations established themselves more in keeping with the massive and impersonal style of urbanism. Others took on a more personal form, catering to the style of the smaller primary group. Even others were organized institutionally as reactions to urbanism.

The Beginning of Urban Church Decline

The very urbanism which opened the way for new things and

created an atmosphere for church growth, also developed to the point where this freedom took its toll. The secularism which emerged had a reverse effect upon church life causing occasional decline during this period. Urban social change especially in older cities also began to produce such drastic change as to throw the whole inner city church life out of kilter and precipitate a rate of decline which in time has proved to be all but fatal for the traditional central city church.

A Model: Houston Southern Baptist Churches

Although no denomination can reflect the total growth patterns of urban churches in a given city, the Southern Baptist churches of Houston will give a good picture of what was happening in this era. Because Southern Baptists traditionally have been a white Southern denomination, they will not reflect in this period the variety which they now reflect. This is especially true with regard to such types as the ethnic church.

In terms of more traditional types, however, Houston Baptist churches reflect a rather typical picture. The first church began in 1841 and was the only church in the town for over fifty years (at least no Baptist churches survived from that period). Two other churches were started in the nineties: Tabernacle in 1892 and Liberty in 1896. The two decades after the turn of the century witnessed the typical development of residential congregations. Beginning in 1903, ahead of these community churches, was South Main which developed into a classic uptown church type. Leading the way of the emerging residential churches was First Heights in 1904 followed by Calvary in 1905, West End in 1906, and Emmanuel in 1907. In 1908 Baptist Temple was organized and in time developed into a large residential type. Other typical residential types followed: Magnolia Park, North Main, and Mt. Houston in 1912, Woodland and Harbour in 1916, and Cochran Street in 1917. In 1918 Park Place was constituted and has in time also developed into a large residential type. In 1926 the First Mexican Baptist Church was organized, though at that time it was affiliated with a separate Mexican Baptist body. In 1927 the Second Baptist Church was formed, and it immediately developed into a typical uptown type. Thus in this early period, Houston Baptists had developed Old First, two typical uptown church types, and two typical large residential church types. It developed typically a significant number of neighborhood churches which in time were to develop into typical models of small and medium-size congregations. For a period of time Tabernacle developed into a more typical people's church type. However, that type was to be found more typically among independent Baptist churches.

Actually in this early period, the Houston churches were a part of an association which comprised an area of some fifty miles in circumference. The oldest of the churches was First Galveston, begun in 1840, a year before First Houston. No other churches were started in this area outside of Houston for the next thirty-five years. Then ten churches were begun before the turn of the century.

Before World War II, there were some 130 churches in the association with some sixty of these being in Houston proper.[4] We shall illustrate in the next chapter three significant developments in the Baptist work in the Houston area after World War II: (1) the phenomenal growth of new churches, (2) the drastic changes in the older churches, and (3) the development of a new and varied pattern of church life.

Notes

[1] C. Peter Wagner, *Frontiers in Missionary Strategy* (Chicago: Moody Press, 1971), pp. 181–83.

[2] Robert Lee, *Stranger in the Land: A Study of the Church in Japan* (London: Lutterworth Press, 1967), pp. 55–132.

[3] Douglas Jackson, *The Downtown Church;* Robert Wilson, *Methodism in the Inner City;* Murray Leiffer, *Five Residential Churches* (Philadelphia: Department of City Work, Division of National Missions, Board of Missions of the Methodist Church, 1958).

[4] *Minutes of the One Hundred and Third Annual Session of Union Baptist Association,* 1943.

5 The Urban Present

The dramatic changes created by the current urban crisis have deeply influenced urban church life. While the various traditional urban congregational types have continued from the era of the metropolis, many new factors are exerting influences which are changing them. In addition, earlier urban forms of the church have been revived, and new forms are emerging. This has caused some to change the traditional classification of congregations.

In his general typology, Ezra Earl Jones sees six basic types of Christian congregations: Old First Church downtown, the neighborhood church, the metropolitan-regional church, the special purpose church, the small-town church, the open country church, and churches in transition. He sees these as still viable types, but he also sees the emergence of additional types in the period between 1940 and 1970. These new types are all urban congregations. They are the "mission" congregation, the minority congregation, the style-centered congregation, the new congregation in the redeveloped area, the traditional suburban congregation, and the ecumenical congregation.[1]

Lyle Schaller departs from the traditional classification and develops six new types: the church on the plateau (the four levels of numerical growth), the ex-neighborhood church, the ex-rural church, the teenage church, the youth to maturity church, and the *Saturday Evening Post* church.[2] The two "ex-type" churches reveal the urban influence on traditional types. The *Saturday Evening Post* church is another name for the transitional church. The two other designations reflect age descriptions of churches.

The Changing Urban Church Scene

It is clear from these two examples of new classifications that the church today has undergone some drastic changes as a result of the rapid urban development since World War II. Let us look first at some of the general trends and then at a broader classification of essentially new congregational types which illustrate how churches are growing in fresh and exciting ways.

The Blending of Congregational Types

An obvious feature of modern urban congregational life is the tendency for traditional congregations to blend in type. One major reason for this of course is the drastic change in the areas where churches are located. We observe the tendency of downtown churches to become transitional like the inner city churches, or the tendency of former neighborhood churches to become regional in character, or the tendency of the suburban churches to become like the former stable central city residential churches.

The Regionalization of the Church

With the radical changes in communities and the breakup of a sense of community in the traditional neighborhoods, few churches today have a sense of neighborhood identity which characterized urban church communities of the past. Thus, the traditional neighborhood church has almost disappeared. Churches seem more and more today to reflect a transgeographical character.

Besides the rapid and radical changes in the traditional communities, there is another reason for this phenomenon. There is a tendency in an urban society for "place" to mean less and less. People today usually achieve community transgeographically, that is, vocationally, professionally, avocationally, recreationally, religiously, and so forth. As urbanism intensifies, the social significance of geography declines. A generation which in the main has not experienced such phenomena as "the old home place" sentiment is not apt to develop that sentiment about the church. The more urbanized mentality of pragmatism prevails. People go to church where they want to, and generally they do not feel necessarily any obligation to the congregation in their own geographic community. Most of the some one thousand Southern Baptist congregations in California are essentially regional, and the main reason for this is that virtually all of them were begun in the era of the megalopolis since World War II.

The Shifting of Church Leadership

We have observed earlier the significant leadership role traditionally played in denominational life by the downtown church, the uptown church, the large residential church, and sometimes the university church. In areas where these churches have declined, the shift in denominational leadership has moved to the new emerging large suburban church. Where these central city churches remain strong, the emerging suburban giants tend to share equally as leaders in the denomination. In the North and East this trend has been more pronounced than in the South and Southwest.

The Continuing Central City Exodus

The exodus from the central city on the part of the strong and prestigious churches continues despite the effort on the part of the denominations to try to keep these churches in their traditional locations. The trend continues even in cities where the downtown area is experiencing significant renewal and expansion. Houston is a good example of this. This means a change in image for the former downtown churches. In many cases also it means leaving a significant spiritual vacuum in the vital downtown area. Although these congregations may continue to be leaders in the city, the symbolism and the impact are not the same.

The Deepening Crisis of the Transitional Church

The crisis of the church in transition which began in the metropolitan era, has reached tragic proportions in recent years. Between 1950 and 1975, some 2,330 Southern Baptist churches died. The churches in the changing central cities accounted for a significant proportion of these. The others were primarily from declining rural areas or a result of rural-urban migration. In the Southern Baptist stronghold of Atlanta, there was a 26.6 percent loss of churches from 1965 to 1975. It is estimated that 2,000 Southern Baptist churches in urban transitional areas are facing a serious crisis.[3]

In a special Home Mission Board study (Southern Baptist Convention) of 5,543 churches, 977 congregations were discovered to be in communities in crisis. These communities are in crisis primarily because of racial and economic changes. The transitional picture was as follows for these communities: 24.5 percent were changing to middle-class black, 19.5 percent to lower-class black, 13.3 percent to Spanish surname, and 22 percent to lower-class white. The other percentages represent other types of transition. The study concluded that these churches were in crisis in their changing communities primarily because their programs were geared exclusively to middle-class whites.[4]

Only the most favorable of circumstances have protected the downtown, uptown, people's, university, and large residential congregations. Most any of these congregational types therefore could become transitional. Indeed many have. Even ethnic churches have suffered from transition, but usually with a somewhat different set of circumstances. The congregation which has suffered the most from transition and is therefore the most typical of the transitional types is the former medium-sized residential church. It has come now more commonly to be referred to as the inner city church. This is significant because this type congregation a generation ago constituted the majority of the congregational types in a given city and therefore the backbone of a given denomination's congregational witness in that city. Many, and in some cities most, of these churches have either moved, died, or merged or they are presently in decline. In some cases that decline may be modest, however. The inner-city churches which are doing well today have usually first suffered a decline.

A significant number of downtown churches are doing quite well, and some are holding their own. A few are enjoying remarkable growth. However, many, if not most, have been in trouble.

The drastic changes in the downtown area and the extensive development of the suburbs have had a negative effect on many downtown churches. With the shifting of the retail shops from the central business district to the suburban centers, the downtown has become a less attractive place, and its institutions have suffered from this. Decaying neighborhoods near the central business district have driven people farther from the downtown area and given them less incentive to drive back to church. Newer residential and suburban churches are becoming increasingly attractive to Old First members. These and many other internal and external problems have brought significant decline to many downtown churches. The result has been that some have moved, some have merged with other churches, and some have died. The picture is a mixed one. Because Old First has had a tremendous backlog of prestige, talent, and money (endowment in some cases), it has been able in many cases to resist the social change which has been fatal to sister neighborhood churches in transition. Though in a sense all central city churches tend to be in some kind of transition, Old First does not fit the typical picture of transition because of its uniquely urban character and history. There is one way Old First is not like the cathedral; it stands or falls on its own merit without the state or diocese on which to fall back.

The Renewal of Central City Churches

The last decade has witnessed some reversal of the discouraging picture of the transitional church. Renewal has come at two levels, both at the beginning and after the crisis of the transitional process. Not only have many downtown and uptown churches resisted or reversed this declining trend, some of the more vulnerable inner city churches have also. Chapter 10 will deal exclusively with this problem, and we shall have opportunity there to illustrate some of these inspiring cases.

The Explosion of the Suburban Church

Because suburbanization has been one of the most significant features of the current urban development, it is not surprising to see the rapid growth of suburban congregations. In some cases the suburban churches have developed as rapidly as the suburbs. The growth has come from three major sources: (1) the movement of central city churches into the suburbs, (2) the suburbanization of smaller town, village, and open country churches which have been enveloped in the suburban process, and (3) the creation of new congregations. Because the suburbs now include both the working class and the professional class, churches tend to assume these basic orientations. Both types tend to be regional. The working-class type tends to resemble the traditional people's church, and the professional type the uptown or larger residential church. This is true even when the churches do not become large. In some cases, growth of suburban churches has been phenomenal. It is this growth which has largely compensated for the decline of rural and inner city churches.

The Multiplication of Ethnic Churches

As central cities have increasingly become the home of ethnic minorities, ethnic churches have emerged to serve their constituency and fill the vacuum left by the abdication of the white churches. In addition to blacks who have migrated from the farms and Mexicans who have come from Mexico, the inner city has also witnessed a large influx of Asians and Latin Americans. Communities in California that experienced a transition from white to black and Spanish surnames a generation ago are now beginning to experience a new transition from black/Spanish to Asian. This has brought internationals to central cities in unprecedented numbers. Partly through the vision and strategy of aggressive denominations and partly through the enterprise of the new ethnics themselves, there has been a multiplication of ethnic and language churches in the central cities of the United States in the last few years. In the last five years over 500 Southern Baptist ethnic (or language) churches were started among some twenty language groups. In 1976 alone, 220 such congregations were started among ten different language groups.[5] In the three year period, between 1973 and 1975, seven Korean Southern Baptist churches were started in California alone.[6] The gospel is preached in over twenty different languages each week in Southern Baptist churches of California.

The Growing Prominence of the Black Church

The black community is unique among the ethnic communities of the American city. The blacks alone were brought to the United States against their will. After the Emancipation Proclamation, they still did not share in the mainstream of the American dream. As the urban and agrarian revolution forced them from their tenements on the farms and into the cities in search of jobs and in hope of a new and better life, they occupied the only territory available to them, the older residential areas of the inner city. Because blacks had developed a profound sense of community partly as a survival mechanism in a white man's world, the inner city became not simply their residence, not simply their home, but their "turf." From the beginning, the blacks slowly, quietly, and confidently built the institution which of all institutions was most their own—the church. They knew what the church was. They knew how to build it. Next to the family, it was the deepest expression of their survival-style. Indeed to many it was their family, their home. From their rural roots the community and church had been essentially one. Thus the most indigenous of all institutions in the black ghetto is the church.

As blacks became urbanized, they became better educated. They produced outstanding leaders. Out of the black ghettos of America have come some of the leading citizens in education, politics, sports, and entertainment. The church has been prominent in developing these leaders. The black pastor today enjoys a much higher community status than his white counterpart.

The American civil rights movement which shook the world had its origin in the black community. Troublesome revolutionary movements and violent outbreaks among the desperates in the black ghettos have brought the nation more than once to its knees. One simple fact—a black majority in the city—has given the black community a power base in the political arena. Black ministers' groups often speak with significant power in cities across the United States. The black church dots the landscape of the city, and some of the most prestigious congregations in America are predominantly black. With a strong sense of community identity, the black pastor and his congregation are looming large on the emerging urban horizon. By and large in most central cities, especially the older ones, the black churches are consistently the greatest in number, the largest in size, the most solvent economically, the most relevant socially, and the most influential politically.

The Recovery of the House Church

We observed earlier that the most definitive structure of the early church was the house church. Even though some form of the mass public meeting was essential to the communication of the gospel in the cities, the specific form of the structure was not consistent: the temple, the synagogue, the marketplace, the open plaza. However, when it came to the regular ongoing context for the life of the church, it was consistently the homes where the church met.

In the wake of the modern urban revolution, this concept and this style have been recovered. It seems clearly to be a part of the whole small group movement which is sweeping the world. They range from various "touch" groups, which are more psychological in nature, to the religious groups, of which the house church is an example. Actually what is happening is the development of a special expression of the primary group. It is a response to the massiveness and anonymity of normative public life in an urban society. It is more than this, however, for it is not simply the classical primary group. It is not normally related to family, vocation, avocation, or other such basic functions which seem to influence the major styles of the primary groups. These small groups are usually either ideological or personal. They are built around an idea or a search. They are therefore in that sense spiritual, though in some cases not religious in the strictest sense. However, some are profoundly so, and the house church is the best example of this. In that case, idea and quest are united.

Donald R. Allen in his study of the house church illustrates how the apostolic form of the house church has been recovered in the twentieth century. It was first noticeable in Europe, mostly in England and Scotland during the closing years of World War II. Even though all types of house churches have emerged in response to the pressures of the modern society, the circumstances surrounding the emergence of these groups and the occasions which gave birth to them have varied. In Halton, London, it was the failure of normal parish life to provide the ingredients necessary for a meaningful spiritual life. In Scotland it was the absence of the quality of Christian fellowship which could support a ministry of the laity. In the Iona community it was the concern of the church for the industrial community.

Allen observes the spread of the house church movement to the United States in the 1960s. The Church of Our Savior in Washington, D. C., was a pioneer. He emphasizes the wide variety of styles and illustrates the basic models from a Catholic church in Claremont, California; the Valley United Church of Christ, Concord, California; and his own Trinity Presbyterian Church of Harrisonburg, Virginia.[7]

Another excellent example of the development of house churches is in Singapore. The Singapore Baptist Convention has adopted a "house church strategy" of new work in order to penetrate the high-rise apartments where most of the people live. Despite the relative newness of the program, there is today a new house church for each traditional church in the Convention.[8]

Growth Through New Church Types

There has been more than a change in general patterns of growth and decline in the modern urban era. A number of new church types have appeared which do not clearly fit the traditional types created in the extensive congregational development of the last urban era. There has been more than a tendency of types to blend. Essentially new types have emerged. It is important that a significant degree of church growth today is coming from these new forms of urban church life.

The Regional Church

Ezra Earl Jones lists among his church types the "metropolitan-regional church." In this type he sees essentially the same model which we have described as the uptown church. He sees it as existing in suburbia as well as in the city. He also views it as large and assuming the traditional role of the downtown church with its wealth and status.[9] However, in the modern period there has emerged a significant number of churches which are neither large nor prestigious, but at the same time are definitely regional. They do not draw a significant number of their members from any one community, not even necessarily the neighborhood in which the church is located in some instances. This church may be one which has moved from another location: usually downtown or a transitional inner city area. In the case of the relocation of the former downtown church, it may simply be continuing its traditional metropolitan style. The former inner-city congregation now in a suburb probably has taken on its regional nature since arriving in its new setting. In some cases, however, totally new congregations have assumed this regional character from the beginning. These churches may not be metropolitan in the classic Old First sense, drawing from the whole metropolis. In fact most are not. However, they do draw from a wide range of communities within a given general area. The one most distinguishing feature of such a church is not its size, not the economic status of its members, not the particular type of urban geography in which its building is located—but the regional character of its membership.

The Church on the Rural-Urban Fringe

Another type of congregation which was beginning to emerge in the latter part of the metropolis and which has become a clearly new type in the modern period is the church on the fringes of urban penetration of the country. It has created a different kind of transition from the inner city situation—a kind of transition in reverse. As the metropolis reached out to envelop the rural hinterlands, many older rural, village, and town areas were surrounded by new suburban developments. Many of these new suburbanites simply established suburban churches in the heart of their particular community.

The most interesting development is the former open country, village, and town church which have found themselves invaded by the new suburbanites. In some cases these people have come from the open country, village, or small-town communities in other areas, and they simply have gravitated to the congregations of their choice, fitting in quite well. However, some of them are from central cities and tend to be more urbane and progressive in their thinking. Consequently their advent into these established churches has tended to threaten the older members.

Both the size of the invasion and the attitude of the invaders cause no small concern in many churches. Many if not most of these churches have taken it in stride. These areas, existing a long time near the city, have been accustomed to city ways. Many of the people, in terms of their life-style, were already essentially urbanized. Indeed, many have been commuting into or near to the city for their jobs. The result has been that, despite the special adjustment problem, many of these churches have become rather typically suburban in their mentality and style. Not a few have failed to make the adjustment, however, and have become ghettoized. Some no longer exist, having conceded to their more adaptable sister congregations near them.

The Megachurch

Even though large churches are not unique to the recent urban scene, there has never been a time when we have had so many large churches and when we have had such a significant number of giant congregations. There is a growing community of churches today with multiplied thousands of members.

The Garden Grove Community Church, which is just a little over twenty years old, has over 7,000 members and averages over 9,000 persons in their Sunday services. Its church facility is not located on a "site" but on a "campus" of twenty-two acres. Nine ordained ministers lead a staff of eighty people.[10]

Two other congregations which have emerged in recent years are the charismatic communities of Melodyland Christian Center of Anaheim and Calvary Chapel of Costa Mesa. Although they are "centers" as well as churches, they are nonetheless congregations. The Sunday morning service attendance at Melodyland is around 10,000 and at Calvary Chapel around 8,000.[11]

The controversial People's Temple of San Francisco, which started in the small northern California community of Redwood Valley a few years ago and later moved to the city, boasts 15,000 members. It has an incredible network of ministries most of which are so phenomenal in scope that they can only be described as "enterprises."

One of the most phenomenal churches of today is the First Baptist Church of Hammond, Indiana. Although not a new church, this congregation has enjoyed most of its growth in recent years under the leadership of Jack Hyles as pastor. In 1974 the average Sunday School attendance was 13,505. On one special occasion, the church had 30,000 in attendance at Sunday School.[12]

Space would not permit the description of other large churches, some of which have enjoyed almost incredible growth in recent years: First Baptist of Dallas; Houston; Jacksonville, Florida; Van Nuys, California. Others are North Phoenix Baptist Church of Phoenix, Arizona; the Thomas Road Baptist Church of Lynchburg, Virginia; Rex Humbard's Cathedral of Tomorrow; the Coral Ridge Presbyterian Church of Fort Lauderdale, Florida; Temple Baptist, Detroit; Akron Baptist Temple, Akron, Ohio; The First Assembly of God, Oklahoma City; First Methodist Church, Houston; Concord Baptist Church of Brooklyn. In America the congregational giants run into the thousands and the "super churches" almost into the hundreds.

However, not all of the super churches and church facilities are in the United States. Anyone visiting Seoul, Korea, will be impressed with the Yung Nak Presbyterian Church whose sanctuary of 2,400 is filled to capacity for three Sunday morning services with overflow crowds served by closed circuit television in an auxiliary chapel. But the Yung Nak Church is not the largest of the four hundred churches in Seoul. That honor goes to an Assembly of God church, the Yoido Island Full Gospel Central Church. This church family of 30,000 attends Sunday services in its facility of 8,000 in four shifts of approximately 8,000 each. A staff of sixty full-time ministers directs the work of over 1,300 unpaid "shepherds," each of whom oversees a small house church group. The incredible thing is that the pastor, Yonggi Cho, started this church with only a handful in 1958.[13]

The largest church auditorium in the world is in Sao Paulo, Brazil. It seats 25,000 and houses the Brazil for Christ Church of that city. The church with the largest membership is the Jotabeche Methodist Pentecostal Church of Santiago, Chile. This congregation, which is served by a hundred pastors, operates with a "satellite" style where the members attend the mother congregation in shifts once a month and function the rest of the time in their satellite daughter groups, in the pattern of the Yoido Island Church of Seoul. The Sao Paulo church also operates on the satellite principle.[14]

Some of the most phenomenal church growth in the world today is taking place in Africa. Africa has many examples of the megachurch. One of these is the Castors Grace Brethren Church of Bangui, the capital city of the Central African Republic. Organized in 1954, the church averages over 5,000 in its Sunday morning service. In its structure it also operates on the satellite principle, one mother congregation and seven daughter satellites.[15] Beside such more phenomenal models, it is common for African churches to average 1,000 to 2,000 in their services, as evidenced by the Baptist churches in the cities of Nigeria.

As is obvious from the above, some of the megachurches are really microdenominations. They have all the earmarks of an incipient denomination. This is especially true of some of the nondenominational churches, but it is also true of such denominational churches as the Garden Grove Community Church and the People's Temple of San Francisco. Some of the megachurches, however, are denominational and in no way follow this pattern.

The Base-Satellite Church

We have seen above how the Jotabeche church of Santiago, the Yoido Island Church of Seoul, and the Brazil for Christ Church of San Paulo use satellite styles of church structures. Not all the "super churches" operate with this style, but some do. There are numerous varieties within this basic style, but the essential principle is the same. There is the large mother congregation housed within a large facility. It becomes a base of outreach. The satellite groups may range from small cell groups to rather large semiautonomous congregations. In some cases this is simply a facilitating way of handling a large group. In other cases this becomes a definite strategy of outreach. In the latter case it becomes desirable or advantageous, for it is only through a satellite that a church is able to penetrate certain communities. There may be a language or cultural barrier. In some cases the satellite groups may come in regularly to the mother church. In some situations, the smaller groups come in once a month for the Lord's Supper or fellowship as is the practice of the Second Baptist Church of Little Rock. In some cases the satellite congregation as such never shares in a service at the mother church. Some of the satellites are simply small congregations. Some are Bible study groups, prayer groups, or Christian sensitivity groups without a "content" agenda. Still others may be primarily ministries such as a Christian house for drug rehabilitation or a convalescent home ministry. Not all of these base-satellite churches are megachurches.

The Federated Church

A number of churches which grew out of the Jesus Movement and which were countercultural in their beginning, have developed a modified form of the base-satellite style. There is a fundamental difference, however, for they achieve this style without a traditional church facility as the base. In fact, the "base" grew out of a proliferation of house churches which were formed from Christian houses. After the groups grew through these home ministries, they rented facilities for their larger celebration services on Sunday. Because the larger entity was created by the numerous smaller ones and is more of a celebration occasion than a "mother-base," this model might be called more properly a "federated church." In 1976 the Church of the Open Door of Marin County and San Francisco had twenty-six Christian houses which were instruments of both evangelism and ministry. They met for their Sunday services at the Carpenter's Hall, a rented facility in San Rafael. A book store, thrift shop, and other ministries as well as the houses have been a part of the chain of satellites which have made up this church community.[16] The Grace Church of Marin is a comparable type.

The Multicongregational Church

Another form of church style which is becoming increasingly popular is the multicongregational church. Actually more correctly, it is a multicongregational institution. A good example of this is the Nineteenth Avenue Baptist Church of San Francisco which houses a multicultural English-speaking church, the Mandarin Chinese Baptist Church of San Francisco, and a Japanese mission. All of these meet on Sunday in the same general facility and an Estonian mission meets in the facility once a month. The groups are separate and distinct congregations but share the common facilities through an ingenious arrangement which is just short of remarkable in light of the limited nature of these facilities. The legal work is in the making for each of the separate religious institutions also to constitute as one California legal religious corporation built on the concept of the shared facilities. A much more common model is where only two congregations share the same facility.

The Multiethnic Church

In addition to the growing number of ethnic churches, many of which share facilities with a sister congregation, there is a growing number of churches which have become multiethnic or multicultural. Some have done so without a great deal of consciousness. Others have so developed as a result of a very careful

strategy. In most cases, the congregation begins with one rather
homogeneous group. As the community changes the congregation
becomes more heterogeneous reflecting the varied ethnic makeup
of the community it serves. A multiethnic church may vary from
a fairly even distribution of numbers of various ethnic groups
to a predominance of one, with a sprinkling of several others.
The one feature which determines a multicultural church is the
style of church life which addresses the various needs of its multiethnic constituents. The most obvious changes or adjustments
have come in the style of worship, the most noticeable perhaps
being the music program of the church.

The Exurban and Rurban Church

We have made extensive reference earlier to the development
of exurban and rurban communities as a recent phenomenon.
The exurban community because of its eliteness has not developed
the number and variety of congregations which characterize the
larger more middle-class suburbs. There are two basic reasons
for this: the relative smallness of the exurban communities and
the less inclined church orientation of the upper class. Nevertheless, churches are emerging in these exurban communities, reflecting the general eliteness typical of the style of the community.

The rurban community is so new it has not had time to develop
a clear church type. In many cases, rurbanites have united with
older churches of their choice nearby. In some cases new congregations have been started in these areas. Though located in rural
areas, obviously they are not rural churches in the traditional
sense. As these congregations emerge in number, it will be interesting to observe how closely they will mirror the rurban mentality
and how the congregational style will develop in keeping with
that mentality.

The Ecumenical Church

In recent years a number of denominations have developed
ecumenical congregations. This has been more commonly referred
to as the ecumenical parish. The most celebrated of these has

been the East Harlem Protestant Parish. The approach has been for several denominations to pool their resources, primarily in a multiethnic, transitional setting, for the staffing of a church with a ministry relevant to the needs of the community. The congregation often functions as a center as well as a congregation. It usually has a strong community orientation. In most cases it has been an experiment. There have been varying degrees of success. The East Harlem Protestant Parish provided the inspiration, data, and philosophy for two of the most helpful studies on the urban church to come out of the sixties: George W. Webber's *God's Colony in Man's World* and *The Congregation in Mission.*

The Relocated Church in a Redeveloped Area

Growing out of the urban renewal programs of the fifties and sixties were many redevelopment areas. Slums were cleared in the inner city areas near the downtown section of major cities. Sometimes these areas provided space for new elite communities downtown, usually in high-rise towers such as those in Chicago and Detroit. In some cases these areas provided low-income housing for the inner-city poor, many of whom had been displaced by the urban renewal programs. In such situations property was provided (for a price) for select churches to relocate in the redevelopment area. In some cases churches which were formerly located in the area have relocated in the redeveloped community. However, because of the time factor (a church was required to remain in limbo for several years) and the expenses, it became advantageous in most cases for the displaced churches simply to relocate elsewhere as soon as possible. Because of the cost, such a program has called for denominational support. Often a completely new work has been started in these relocated areas under denominational auspicies.

Special Purpose Church

In a number of situations, denominations have developed special interest churches in various urban settings. It may be a language church or a church started on behalf of a special social group.

In certain instances a denomination may develop a center for some special need in connection with a church. There may be an experiment with a storefront church or a house church. Sometimes one denomination makes a church facility available to another at an attractive price, and the latter has placed a strong leader in the situation because the circumstances and potential seem to have justified it.

The Rural Church in an Urban World

In addition to what we have called the rurban church, the modern urban age has brought into being another phenomenon— a changed rural church. It is what Lyle Schaller has called, "The Ex-Rural Church." The rural church today, by and large, is not the rural church of the past. Its setting may be as rural as ever in terms of geography, but it has not been able to avoid the impact of urbanism. It may consciously try to resist the new ideas and ways which this urbanization imposes, but it cannot escape the impact created by such influences as communication and transportation. In some cases, these influences have created an environment which has enabled rural churches to spark a kind of growth which they have never known.

In other cases, especially in areas where new resort communities have been created near old or rural communities, churches have been able to change with the new style and become a more urban-oriented resort-type church. Other open country and village churches which have not had these special influences have nevertheless yielded to the directions of the times and have gradually changed to accommodate the mood of the dominant influences of the land.

The Life-style Church

Every one has a life-style, of course, and every church has its own style and personality. However, we have come to use this term to refer to people whose life-style is a significant departure from the traditional norms. The beatniks of the fifties and the hippies of the sixties are perhaps the most graphic examples. A life-style church is one which departs in its style from the traditional patterns of most congregations. It may also be one whose members are those whose life-styles are basic social deviations. The controversial Glide Memorial Church of San Francisco is a good example of the former, and the countercultural groups growing out of the Jesus movement are a good example of the latter. These groups have had a strong influence, especially through new forms of music, across the lines of most of the mainstream denominational churches.

The Houston Model Updated

In the last chapter we observed the interesting growth of Houston Southern Baptist churches from their beginning in 1841 to World War II. The continuing story is even more interesting. It helps to illustrate a number of typical and significant developments in urban church life since then. In this recent period, four new associations were created out of the original territory of Union Association, leaving the association with only the greater Houston area. Despite this, the growth has been so marked that today there are 220 churches in the association, despite the losses to the new associations. There are sixty-eight churches with over 1,000 members. The five largest churches have a combined membership of 33,000.

Houston illustrates the phenomenal growth of suburban churches and the consequent sharing in leadership of the new suburban giants with the older leading churches in the city. Most of the growth has come in suburban areas, even though these churches are usually in the city limits because Houston still has room to expand, not being land and water "locked" as are so many large cities: Detroit, Chicago, San Francisco, and others. The rapid emergence of the large suburban church is illustrated by Willow Meadows which was organized in 1958 and has over 3,600 members, and Tallowood which was organized in 1962 and has over 4,200 members. Tallowood led all the churches in Sunday School attendance in 1976.

Other typical developments should be noted. Old First and

Second, classic downtown and uptown types, moved from their original locations and have therefore forfeited these traditional roles. Second is still a leader, being fourth in membership in the association. However, despite its more "favorable" new location, its attendance has not returned to its peak of 1955. First Church has enjoyed phenomenal growth in recent years after a marked decline in the late sixties. With over 9,000 members, it is now taking its place among the emerging megachurches.

Uptown South Main has remained, has enlarged and enriched its outreach and ministry, and is as strong as ever. It is third in Sunday School attendance only to the two more "favorably" located First and Tallowood.

Baptist Temple, the largest of the residential churches for decades, with a Sunday School comparable to the largest in the city, has shown some signs of the effect of urban transition. However, it is still unusually strong for a city residential church, averaging over 800 in Sunday School last year.

Houston also illustrates the transition of congregations from rural to suburban. White Oak, once a small country church out from Houston, has become a typical suburban church. In 1942 it averaged ninety-seven in Sunday school, in 1976 over four hundred. The Fairbanks Church, farther out, is another example. Its Sunday School attendance has tripled in this period.

The changes in racial composition and ethnic makeup have been marked. There are now Chinese, Korean, Japanese, Vietnamese, and Arabic-speaking churches or departments within churches. Within the last decade over a dozen Spanish-speaking churches have been added to the association, bringing the total to nineteen. There are now thirteen black churches, and a few multiethnic churches. Thirty-five percent of the churches have black members. This is especially noteworthy in light of the strongly homogeneous character of the churches in the past.

An example of the innovative church is well illustrated by the West Memorial Church. Untraditional and strongly ministry-oriented, every room in its new church facility has a multipurpose function. Now the church is developing a base-satellite style after the model of the Yoido Island Church of Seoul, where the small house church concept will be a marked feature.

Another typical development characteristic of the modern urban scene is illustrated from the suburban city of Pasadena and its First Baptist Church. Pasadena in its relation to Houston illustrates the city as megalopolis. First Baptist illustrates the growing prominence of the suburban city church in the community of leading congregations in the modern megalopolis. With over 5,000 members, it is the third largest church in Union Association.

Despite the encouraging picture of growth, Houston Baptist churches, with all of their strength, have experienced a marked decline among their once stable and strong residential churches which are now experiencing transition. Because the consistent strength of a Southern Baptist church is usually best measured by its average Sunday School attendance, the following will illustrate what has happened in this period.[17]

AVERAGE SUNDAY SCHOOL ATTENDANCE
Traditionally Strong Medium-sized Residential Churches

	1943	1955	1965	1977
Calvary	426	345	113	— *
First, Heights	613	621	444	123
Magnolia Park	532	500	276	146
Trinity	615	416	240	350
West End	665	892	468	265
Texas Avenue	350	352	184	80
Woodland	576	490	535	201

* Disbanded

Note that Heights and West End were still growing in 1955. Note also the surge of new life by Trinity. The overall picture of these representative churches, however, reflects the type of decline typical of central city churches in recent years.

In addition to Calvary a number of churches have disbanded. Most of them have sold their facilities to black congregations.

Some of the churches which have sold to black churches have moved to new locations and have taken new names.

Reasons for Growth

The Mood of the Times

The background for much of the church growth today comes from a kind of backlash—a reaction against the materialism and secularism of the day. The youth counterculture well symbolizes this. At its heart, it has been essentially a spiritual movement. All over the world there have been deep stirrings within the soul of man, and as a result there has been a new surge of spirituality. Some of it has been woefully misguided, but much of it has been well-directed and channeled.

Spiritual Renewal

Recent times have witnessed both the birth of new forms of church life and the renewal of old forms. There has been a new appreciation for the Bible. The recovery of the biblical teachings on the Holy Spirit and the gifts, however abused some of it has been, has been a decisive factor in new growth. The renewed emphasis upon discipleship is playing a major role. Soul searching on the part of church people, pastors, denominational leaders, and theologians over the inner city church crisis has led us into a new day.

Inspired old churches such as First Baptist, San Antonio and Walnut Street Baptist, Louisville, situated in the midst of deep hurt, have in turn inspired others by the thrilling ways they have applied the whole gospel to the whole man. We are breaking out of our old structures, out of our narrow and limited ways of perceiving and doing things.

Creative Use of Methods

Mass evangelism is more effective than ever, and it is true the world over. Billy Graham preached to over a million at one time in an open meeting in Seoul in 1973. At the same time, our generation under the Holy Spirit's guidance has found fresh and creative ways of penetrating homes and hearts with the Christian message. Literature in almost unlimited varieties is a vital force. Radio, television, the computer, advertising, numerous new approaches to audiovisuals, and other means of the times are playing an increasing role in the spread of the faith.

The Paradoxical Picture

The phenomenal growth of churches in some areas has been matched by a tragic decline in others. Modern urban life therefore dramatically reflects that perennial paradox of the city so far as church life is concerned. Even the Baptist empire of Houston has not escaped some of this tragedy. Despite a continuing decline by some, churches are beginning to make the transition, and the death of Houston churches has virtually stopped. This is a decided reversal from the late sixties, and it points to an encouraging trend.

Notes

[1] Ezra Earl Jones, *Strategies for New Churches* (New York: Harper and Row, Publishers, 1976), pp. 19–26, 35–43.

[2] Lyle Schaller, *Hey, That's Our Church* (New York: Abingdon Press, 1975).

[3] B. Carlisle Driggers, *The Church in the Changing Community: Crisis or Opportunity* (Atlanta: Home Mission Board, 1977), pp. 15–16.

[4] Don F. Mabry, *A Study of Churches in Communities in Crises in Metropolitan Associations in the Southern Baptist Convention, 1973* (Atlanta: Home Mission Board, 1974), pp. 5–13.

[5] *Annual of the Southern Baptist Convention,* 1973, p. 152; 1974, p. 146; 1975, p. 140; 1976, p. 131; 1977, pp. 117–118.

[6] "Korean Baptist Church Growth." Unpublished paper by Daniel Y. Moon, 1976.

[7] Donald R. Allen, *Barefoot in the Church: Sensing the Authentic Through the House Church* (Richmond, Va.: John Knox Press, 1966), pp. 22–36.

[8] Letter from Russell A. Morris, Chairman Malaysia-Singapore Baptist Mission. August 30, 1977.

[9] Jones, op. cit., pp. 40–41.

[10] C. Peter Wagner, *Your Church Can Grow* (Glendale, CA.: A Division of G/L Publications, 1976), p. 88.

[11] Ibid., p. 66.

[12] Ibid., p. 24.

[13] John Stetz, "The Biggest Little Church in the World," *Church Growth Bulletin* (September, 1976), pp. 78,79.

[14] Wagner, op. cit., p. 91.

[15] Virgil Gerber, "A New Tool for Winning the City," *Church Growth Bulletin*, July, 1976, p. 542.

[16] Richard H. Bruner, "Church of the Open Door," Term Paper, Golden Gate Baptist Theological Seminary, 1976, p. 27.

[17] *Minutes of the Annual Session of Union Baptist Association*, 1943, 1955, 1965, 1977; R. G. Commander, *The Story of Union Baptist Association, 1840–1976* (Houston: D. Armstrong Publishers, 1977).

PART III

Theology: How Churches *Should* Grow

6 A Theology of the City

A theology is a way of viewing things from a God point of view or from a God frame of reference. It is a word from God or a word about God. A theology interprets any subject at hand in light not only of the reality of God but of his nature and purpose. The Bible is the chronicle of the acts of God. It is from its pages that we understand his nature and purpose. The Bible therefore becomes the supreme standard for all our ideas and practices. It follows then that a theology of urban church growth must look to biblical sources for the ingredients out of which its vital principles are to be formed.

A theology of urban church growth must address itself, first of all, to two fundamental questions: (1) What is the attitude of the Bible toward the city? (2) What insight does the Bible furnish into the effect of urbanism upon church growth in the New Testament urban context? An answer to these two basic questions will furnish us with the theological principles which will enable us to construct a theology of healthy growth. In other words, a biblical theology of the city and a biblical theology of urbanism will tell us not only how churches have grown but how they should grow.

The urban theme of the Bible is a very rich one. It furnishes us ample understanding of the city and therefore provides us a guide for discerning both the negative and positive meaning of urban reality. The city is more than geography and artifact, however; it is first and foremost people. It is people who are compelled to structure their lives in terms of the demands of the urban way of life. The Bible has an uncanny way of speaking to that way of life, furnishing us with profound insight into its meaning and its implication for church life in a comlex urban setting. The beautiful thing about the theological principles at work in New Testament church growth is that we do not have to find a way to relate them to the urban setting. The New Testament does this for us.

However, the Bible does not suddenly thrust us into the book of Acts with its marvelous account of church growth. Moreover, it is not the book of Acts which first introduces us to the city. The Old Testament as well as the Gospels have prepared us. The God of the Bible has been at work in the cities from their very beginning. To see how he has been at work—to view the wide panorama of the city in the Bible—will give us the best basis for an understanding of the New Testament context of church growth. We must know the whole city and the whole truth about it. The Bible provides us with this understanding.

The most common popular impression of the Bible is pastoral. Yet the urban theme of the Bible is crucial to an understanding of its message. What is the message conveyed by the vocabulary of the city in Scripture? What is the biblical meaning of the city?

The Context of God's Activity

The word *city* appears 1,227 times in the Bible (RSV). In addition to these general references to the city, there are almost unlimited references to specific cities, especially the significant ones, such as Jerusalem and Babylon. For example, Jeremiah alone makes 137 references to the city or cities and 108 references to Jerusalem and 168 references to Babylon. When we add both general and specific references to the city in the Bible, the number of the references becomes staggering.

The city is essential to the unfolding drama of the biblical story. It was a major social context in which the theological events of biblical message transpired. The first reference to the city in the Bible relates to Cain who was the first city builder (Gen. 4:17). The story of the building of the Tower of Babel had its setting in the city: "The Lord came down to see the city and the tower which the sons of man had built" (Gen. 11:5). The cities of Sodom and Gomorrah figured prominently in the life of Abraham (Gen. 18–19). When the Hebrew people were slaves in Egypt, they built storage cities for the pharaohs (Ex. 1:11). After the Exodus and the people of God finally settled in the land which God had promised them, he instructed them to designate cities of refuge, urban centers which became significant in the lives of the people.

With the coming of David, Jerusalem became the political and religious center of the nation. All of life revolved around that great city. With the division of the nation, Samaria, the urban capital of the Northern Kingdom, vied with Jerusalem in importance as the social center of the nation. In time foreign cities such as Nineveh and Babylon became increasingly important in the history of the Hebrew nation. With the dawning of the New Testament era, the city became even more important as the social context of the unfolding revelation of God to his people.

A Symbol of Evil

The tremendous importance the New Testament places on the city as a strategic position of influence, as well as a prime target for the gospel, agrees with the powerful symbolism which the Bible attaches to the city. The symbolism of the urban motif in the Scriptures is seen both in the descriptive accounts of biblical events and in the prophetic and poetic declarations of biblical ideas. Indeed the symbolic city is always based upon a historical city.

The city seems to get off to a bad start in the Bible. The first urban reference in Genesis is a negative one, associating the building of the first city with the murderer Cain. Jacques Ellul, the French Protestant lay theologian, in his widely acclaimed work, *The Meaning of the City,* says: "The city is the direct consequence of Cain's murderous act and his refusal to accept God's protection. Cain has built a city. For God's Eden he substitutes his own, for the goal given to his life by God, he substitutes a goal chosen by himself—just as he substituted his own security for God's. Such is the act by which Cain takes his destiny on his own shoulders, refusing the hand of God in his life." [1]

Ellul sees in Cain the prototype of all city builders and interprets the whole urban theme of the Bible from this premise. To him the city in the Bible represents the epitome of human rebellion against God, an attempt by man in his pride to construct his own social, political, economic, and even moral defenses in defiance of the will and purpose of God for man.

The developing urban drama of Genesis seems to confirm these early suspicions about the city and thus give credence to the thesis of Ellul. The second urban reference in Genesis describes the building of the city and the Tower of Babel (Gen. 11). It was clearly a gesture of man's pride and arrogance and a direct defiance of God. Both the general language of the account and the specific record of the judgment of God upon Babel in the account make this clear. Here the city is not only a symbol of pride and arrogance but the symbol of the breakdown in communication and the confusion which results from it.

The next reference seems to remove all doubt about the inherent nature of the city as evil. The third city dealt with at length in the book of Genesis is the city of Sodom. The details of this account in Genesis 18 and 19 are quite familiar and its implications are equally familiar. So infamous has the name Sodom become that it continues until today not only as a general synonym for depravity and perversity but also as a technical term used by scholars to designate certain sexual aberrations.

This negative view of the city is not one which is confined to Genesis. The Old Testament prophets seemed equally sensitive to the evil capability of the city and urban life. Micah exclaims: "The voice of the Lord cries to the city—and it is sound wisdom to fear thy name:/'Hear, O tribe and assembly of the city!/Can I forget the treasures of wickedness in the house of the wicked,/ and the scant measure that is accursed?' " (Mic. 6:9–10).

Ezekiel declares: "The land is full of bloody crimes and the city is full of violence" (7:23). And again: "The land is full of blood and the city is full of injustice" (9:9).

The climax of this negative image of the city is seen in the picture of Babylon the great in Revelation 17. She is described in the most repulsive terms conceivable: as the "mother of harlots and of earth's abominations" who is "drunk with the blood of the saints" (17:5–6). But Babylon is a code name for Rome, for Revelation 17:18 states: "The woman that you saw is the great city which has dominion over the kings of the earth."

A Symbol of Good

If the above picture were the only image of the city in the Bible, it would be a discouraging one indeed. However, as paradoxical as it seems, the Bible is just as positive about the city as it is negative.

In Joshua 20 we learn of the Lord's direct order to Joshua to designate certain cities as cities of refuge. The purpose of these cities was to serve as havens for persons guilty of manslaughter where they might flee the "avenger of blood" until a fair hearing could be held. These cities therefore symbolize both mercy and justice. Moreover, they were built, not by any motivation of man, let alone one of man's pride and rebellion against God. These cities were established by direct order from God himself and were therefore of divine motivation and origin.

It is interesting to note how Jacques Ellul, who had already generalized on the meaning of the city from the negative Genesis model, deals with the phenomenon of the cities of refuge. He is forced to admit that this text presents a different view of the city from the one he had earlier established. However, he fails to attach any theological significance to the fact that it was God who ordered the designation of these cities.

Because these cities were designed to protect those who had killed, even though they did so accidentally or in self-defense, Ellul sees the city as retaining its original role. He says: "The city is intimately connected with murder; she is warlike and bloody." [2] He inserts in his discussion of the cities of refuge ideas which have no basis at all in that context. Despite the totally different vein of the ideas connected with these cities in contrast to those in Genesis, Ellul still insists categorically that "the city is the place where man is all-powerful, where he establishes his own justice, opposed to God's will" [3]—though there is not a hint of such ideas in Joshua 20. To the contrary, it is God's justice and God's will, not man's, which are established in these cities. Ellul continues: "and here we have the opposition of the city's walls to God's law expressed in the formula 'an eye for an eye.' But this opposition is just in God's sight and in accordance with God's will." [4]

Ellul seems so determined to keep the city in bad light that he sets God against himself—his law against his will. He seems totally unable to accept the city at face value. He is noticeably silent on the theological implications of the fact that it was God who ordered the designation of these cities, and it was his will, his mercy, and his justice which prevailed there. Moreover, even though he does ascribe peripheral significance to some new ideas about the city found in this text, he tries to force the text to conform to his previously determined and totally negative view of the city. However, he cannot do this without doing violence to the obvious intent, the clear teachings, and the evident principles found in Joshua 20.

We shall not deal here with the critical problems involved in the differences between the urban ideologies of these two Old Testament sources. However, a strong point must be registered for a consideration of the data in Joshua and the many other biblical passages which reflect a positive image of the city. Both negative and positive images—indeed all urban references in the Bible—must be considered in the development of a theology of the city.

Even though the prophets were deeply aware of the potential for evil in the city, they were equally appreciative of the potential for good in the city. Ezekiel, whose negative views of urban life have already been cited, also has some very positive pictures of the city. In the close of his prophecy where he describes the restored city, Ezekiel reaches for a name which would best characterize this restored city. The very last line reveals that name: "And the name of the city henceforth shall be 'The Lord is there'" (Ezek. 48:35). Here the city becomes the very symbol of the presence of God himself.

Isaiah has a similar assessment of this restoration. His emphasis, however, is upon the people, the restored people of God. Like Ezekiel who reaches for the highest name possible for his restored city, Isaiah too reaches for the highest name possible for his restored people. He concludes: "They shall call you the City of the Lord, the Zion of the Holy One of Israel" (Isa. 60:14). The prophet could have paid this restored people no greater compliment than to call them "the City of the Lord."

These glowingly positive images of the city in the Old Testament are not limited to descriptions of restoration. The Hebrew psalmist was especially appreciative of the positive qualities of which urban life was capable. In Psalm 107 he pictures the tragedy of a people having to wander in the wilderness with no city in which to dwell (a striking and daring idea against the background of a strongly Bedouin culture). Of course, this is a reference to the wilderness wanderings of the children of Israel before they settled in the land of Canaan. Nevertheless, this does not in any sense minimize the positive image of the city and urban life which is depicted by the psalmist: "Some wandered in desert wastes, finding no way to a city to dwell in;/hungry and thirsty, their soul fainted within them./Then they cried to the Lord in their trouble, and he delivered them from their distress;/he led them by a straight way, till they reached a city to dwell in./Let them thank the Lord for his steadfast love, for his wonderful works to the sons of men!" (Ps. 107:4–8).

Here the city is portrayed as a place of security and stability and as a place of physical and spiritual prosperity. The city is synonymous with home and community.

When the psalmist sang of the city of Jerusalem, there was almost no limit to the positive language which he employed in the celebrations. Jerusalem was the symbol of God's presence and the ultimate place of worship: "Great is the Lord and greatly to be praised in the city of our God!/His holy mountain, beautiful in elevation,/is the joy of all the earth, Mount Zion, in the far north,/the city of the great King" (Ps. 48:1–2).

The New Testament builds extensively on these affirming concepts of the city in the Old Testament. Not only was apostolic

Christianity an urban movement, its ideology was strongly urban
in its orientation. The New Testament decribes the spiritual pilgrimage not in idyllic terms, but in urban terms. Abraham looked
not for restored Eden but for a city which had foundations whose
builder and maker is God (Heb. 11:10).

The ultimate imagery of the Bible is strongly urban. The final
scenes of the book of Revelation are city scenes. Just as Babylon
the great, the symbolic designation of imperial Rome, represents
the epitome of ultimate evil—so the new Jerusalem, pictured as
a bride adorned for her husband, represents the epitome of ultimate
good. Like Babylon and Rome, Jerusalem is also portrayed as a
woman. Unlike Babylon and Rome, however, she is not pictured
as a repulsive harlot but as the exact opposite—a beautiful and
chaste bride adorned for her wedding day (Rev. 21:2).

The symbolism of Jerusalem is rich in imagery. Jerusalem became Mount Zion and thus incorporated the ancient idea of equat-
ing God's presence with "the holy mountain." It also incorporated
the garden qualities of the Edenic paradise, though the language
of Eden as such is carefully avoided. This is illustrated in such
passages as Psalm 46:4: "There is a river whose streams make
glad the city of God,/the holy habitation of the Most High."
The book of Revelation employs a similar figure in describing
the New Jerusalem: "Then he showed me the river of the water
of life, bright as crystal, flowing from the throne of God and of
the Lamb through the middle of the street of the city" (Rev.
22:1–2).

The Paradox of Reality

How can the Bible, otherwise marvelous in its unity, portray
such a contradictory picture of the city? It can do so because of
its fidelity to history and to life. The biblical paradox of the city
is the paradox of reality. The reality of both evil and good in
the city is a fact of urban life: ancient, historical, contemporary.
The city as the ultimate extension of earthly man excites the highest, both of evil and of good, in the spirit of man.

Ellul and others who write from an antiurban bias do not see the full picture of the city—its inherent capacity for both good and evil. Contrary to Ellul, the biblical city is described in divine as well as human terms. In the view of Ellul, the only positive value of the city is as the context of the visitation of God's grace in Christ. This overlooks the many positive images of the city in both the Old and New Testaments. What the city becomes depends upon man and his response to God's redemptive purpose for him on the earth. Judgment upon the city in the Bible was not simply upon the great heathen cities such as Babylon and Rome. Even Jerusalem, when she failed to do God's will and departed from the commandments of God, became the object of his judgment. Isaiah described such a situation: "How the faithful city has become a harlot, she that was full of justice!/Righteousness lodged in her, but now murderers" (Isa. 1:21). Both Isaiah and John in Revelation refer to Jerusalem as Sodom—the ultimate insult (Isa. 1:10; Rev. 11:8).

In his typically plaintive style, Jeremiah depicts the same Jerusalem, but his emphasis is upon the tragedy of a once people-filled city which has now become desolate. Employing a different metaphor from Isaiah, he laments: "How lonely sits the city that was full of people!/How like a widow she has become, she that was great among the nations!" (Lam. 1:1).

The evil in Jerusalem, according to the prophet, was not in her origin as a creation of man's pride and murderous intent, as Ellul contends. Her sin was just the opposite—in becoming evil after she had been good, in becoming the spiritual harlot after originally being the spiritual model of justice and righteousness on the earth.

The Scene and Goal of the Christian Pilgrimage

A biblical theology of the city may be constructed clearly from the ideological content conveyed by the urban theme of the biblical message. The story of the Bible begins in the garden, but it ends in the city. Even though Jerusalem as a spiritual symbol incorporates all the treasured religious ideals of Eden and the sacred mountain, it is nevertheless still the city. And even though the new Jerusalem, like the modern megalopolis with its lingering ruralism, incorporates some of the idyllic qualities of Eden—nevertheless, like the modern megalopolis, it is nonetheless still the city, and profoundly so. The Bible never seeks to return to Eden. Even though the New Testament reaches back to the ancient nomad Abraham for its ideal of faith, it urbanizes that spiritual pilgrimage. Abraham looked for a city. The Bible is primarily history-oriented not nature-oriented. It is never imprisoned in the static cycles of nature. Rather it moves with the dynamic developments of history, retaining what nature-values it is able to adapt and carry meaningfully with it into the ever changing scenes of the emerging city. How incredibly contemporary!

The urbanization of the spiritual pilgrimage in New Testament theology does not mean that the city's realities were idealized away. To the contrary, they were reckoned with totally. The church today must have that same realistic view of the city and urban life. It must accept the city as capable of reflecting both the Joshua model of divine origin with its ideals of mercy and justice and the Babel model of human origin with its realities of pride and confusion. Moreover, it should be open to a recognition that most cities may not reflect strictly either of these two extreme views but probably will demonstrate qualities of both of these classical models. A sound biblical theology of the city must avoid either the tendency of an Ellul to develop a totally negative view of the city or the tendency of a Harvey Cox to develop a totally positive view of the city (as in *The Secular City*). Neither view takes full cognizance of the ideas and implications expressed through the urban language of the Bible.

The city has always been a mixed blessing—the maker and breaker of civilizations. It has always brought to mankind the greatest potential for both the enrichment of life and the destruction of life. As the extension of man, it is capable of becoming the socialized expression of any extremity of which man himself is capable. Subsequent history has verified this paradoxical view of the city in the Bible. The church of the emerging world would do well to recognize this.

In summary, the principles of a biblical theology of the city may be expressed as follows. The city, which is the ultimate extension of earthly man and which is therefore capable of evil and good, is both the scene and goal of the Christian pilgrimage. It is therefore the arena of the Christian mission and consequently the context and strategic base of influence for the planting and development of Christian churches throughout the earth.

Notes

[1] Jacques Ellul, *The Meaning of the City* (Grand Rapids: William B. Eerdmans Publishing Company, 1970), p. 5.

[2] Ibid., p. 93.

[3] Ibid.

[4] Ibid

7 A Theology of Urbanism

It is common for treatises on the urban church to claim that there is no special theology of the church in an urban society which differs from a theology of a church in any society. Such a view seems to be understanding theology in a very limited sense or else has not reckoned with two significant realities: (1) the strongly ruralized nature of formal and popular theology and (2) the fundamental difference between ruralism and urbanism. Of course, the nature of the church does not change, but how the church functions in a given social context is affected by the nature of that social context. For example, it is the nature of the Christian congregation to minister. That function does not change. However, the congregation ministers to a dynamic and mobile society in terms of that dynamism and mobility and not as if it were a static society. A vital theology not only expresses what the Christian faith is, it expresses how it functions in a given social context through church life. If we are to develop an adequate theology of urbanism, we must understand biblical theology in its relation to the basic characteristics of the urban way of life.

Let us therefore consider biblical insights as to the basic dimensions of urbanism and especially note how the dynamic interplay between theology and urbanism determined the pattern of church growth in the New Testament period. Drawing upon what we have observed earlier on the nature of urbanism (chap. 2) and church growth in the New Testament period (chap. 3), let us focus specifically upon the theology of these urban expressions with a view to determining the principles of church growth which emanate from them.

Massiveness

Massiveness is the stuff out of which urbanism is made. We have observed from Jesus, Peter, Philip, and Paul that they understood how to communicate with the masses in the urban setting of their day. Mass evangelism and mass structures of church life were inherent features of New Testament Christianity. The gospel was communicated in a way that was indigenous to the nature of urban life. In other words, that communication was not alien to the patterns of urban life and expression. Therefore the church multiplied and flourished. It not only grew as a result of relating to the patterns of the mass public meeting in its urban environment, but it incorporated that structure into its life and style as an urban institution. The gospel was in no way threatened by this massiveness but expressed itself through it. The living presence which captured the minds and hearts of the early church was the Lord of history who moved with his people in the midst of the masses and through the massive structures of the day.

Anonymity

Inherent in the massiveness of urban life is anonymity or impersonalism. The theological principle by which we are best able to understand the positive aspects of this urban characteristic is the New Testament concept of *agape* love. *Agape* love is impersonal and nonsentimental. It is the kind of love which does not have to know the object of its love and is not emotionally involved with that object. The personal and emotional type of love typical of the village past is not necessary to communicate the love of God in an urban age.

The story of the good Samaritan illustrates this well. Jesus told this story as an illustration of how we should love our neighbor. From every indication the Samaritan did not personally know the person whom he helped. He was not personally or emotionally involved with him. Yet he had compassion on him.

Agape love evokes compassion for a person not because of who he is or what he is—but simply bcause he is a person and because he is in need. *Agape* love demands nothing of its recipient. That is, it requires nothing on his part to evoke that love. The source of *agape* love is wholly in the lover and not the beloved. If there is a need, *agape* love meets that need—no questions asked. Therefore, no matter how impersonal a society becomes, *agape* is relevant and effective.

This is the reason the New Testament describes God's love in terms of *agape*. He loves us not because we are lovely and lovable. He loves us because he is God. The source of his love is within himself and not within us. Indeed it is this God kind of love which is operative in us when we so love. The difference between God and us, of course, is that God knows all and therefore his love is not in that sense impersonal. However, it is not God's specific knowledge about persons which motivates him, according to the Bible, but his loving nature. His love for man is because he is God and not because of his knowledge or lack of knowledge relating to man. What Romans 5:8 is really saying is that God loves us because he is God, and the fact that we are sinners does not keep him from loving us.

Because modern man has brought so much of his rural values with him into his new urban setting, he tends to view much of urbanism in negative terms. While he is compelled by social necessity to operate in a massive, impersonal world, he often views this in a totally unfavorable way. This reactionary attitude needs to be corrected by the positive way in which the New Testament demonstrates the presence of Christian compassion in the impersonal settings of its urban context.

Jesus was not personally acquainted with all of the persons within the multitudes whom he repeatedly addressed. Yet his compassion upon them was authentic, and it was especially emphasized by the Gospel writers. Paul's compassion upon the multitudes in Ephesus was specifically noted by Luke. It is abundantly clear from the New Testament that *agape* love was at work in the mass evangelism of the day. This compassionate evangelism was the first step of church growth. Out of it the Christian congregations emerged and multiplied.

It is in this fundamental realm of impersonalism that we are able to see the paradox of urban life. Anonymity can be a positive and constructive force in one's life. Indeed in the public sphere, it must be if one is to be normative in urban life, as we have observed earlier. However, in the private sphere, it can also have value. There may be freedom from the pressures of the extended family. This liberation may have positive effects, especially if those pressures are non-Christian. To be free from the psychological tyranny of the extended family or small group can indeed be liberating. Freedom from the malicious gossip of small communities is freedom indeed. Often anonymity is a refuge away from the personally stifling and emotionally unhealthy situations of bad personal relations.

This is only one side of the picture, however, for anonymity can be devastating, resulting in social alienation, an identity crisis, and a loss of a sense of belonging. As much as urban man identifies with mass structures as a part of his indigenous urban life-style, and as much as he needs the option of urban anonymity, he also needs personal relations and primary group identity. It is a part of the paradox of the city because it is a part of the paradox of man. The sensory overload of urban multiple stimuli can be more than impersonal, it can be depersonal. It can be depersonalizing.

This is the reason evangelism in the New Testament took the form of an invitation to community: "That which we have seen and heard we proclaim also to you, so that you may have fellowship with us; and our fellowship is with the Father and with his Son Jesus Christ" (1 John 1:3). Evangelism in the New Testament was often a household strategy as in the case of the house of Cornelius and the Philippian jailer. Reaching out to meet the deep need "to belong" on the part of urban man, the early church from the beginning structured itself along family lines. It was the household of God, and for its deepest ongoing nurturing life, it met in the homes, as our previous description of apostolic church life amply illustrated.

This need on the part of urban man for both mass and personal communication the early church understood well. Such an understanding came by a kind of spiritual instinct—a holy discernment which was second nature to the church as an indigenous urban entity. The church "impacted" through mass communication, and it "penetrated" through small house group meetings. Personal and household evangelism paralleled mass evangelism. House churches paralleled mass assemblies. Both were important because both were necessary.

Heterogeneity

An urban society is characterized by pluralism. It is strongly marked by variety. Often this variety is complex. Cities are stratified, divided along economic, racial, and structural lines. Much of the city is a kind of mosaic. However, much of it is integrated, with some communities reflecting a marked variety. This variety and diversity may exist both within smaller and larger units of the urban expression.

The early church understood this. One of the clearest pictures in the book of Acts is how the gospel moved across these diverse lines. The first converts were from among diverse groups: Jews and Gentiles, men and women, Greeks and Romans, rich and poor, intellectual and unlearned. The first churches had this variety in them from the beginning. Even the Jerusalem church was composed of Hellenistic as well as Palestinian Jews. The rich and poor were also together. We shall deal with this later in connection with a discussion of the homogeneous unit principle.

Mobility

From the beginning, biblical faith was mobile. It was formed in the context of the life-style of a nomadic people. Certain places in the Bible had special religious significance, but the God of the Bible was not a "place-God." It is true that in the Temple at Jerusalem God seemed to dwell in a special way; yet this fate cannot obscure the pilgrimage orientation of the biblical faith. With the coming of Christ and the era of the New Testament, the pilgrim understanding of the early Hebrews returned and achieved an even more meaningful expression.

The early churches were at home in the urban centers in which they emerged. At the start Christianity was dynamic, and it moved with a dynamic society—adapting to its changes and penetrating its structures with its message of life.

Modern Protestantism emerged from the social context of rural life. It developed institutionally along static lines. Now that society is being urbanized, the Christian congregation is in crisis. It has been slow to adapt itself institutionally to its changing social context. It needs to recover the dynamism of its primitive roots and restructure itself to serve a mobile and dynamic age. The church must go mobile in mission if it is to relate to a mobile society, and the basis of this mobile style may be found in the dynamism of its faith.

There is a remarkable affinity between the dynamism inherent in the mobility of the urban way of life and the dynamism inherent in the mobility of the Christian pilgrimage. The object of the Christian faith is the living God who leads his pilgrim people on a journey through the city of man ultimately to the city of God. The people of God today can learn a vital lesson in evangelism from the model of the New Testament church. It was essentially a "people" and not "a place," and it moved dynamically in a dynamic culture, spontaneously and creatively developing a capacity for communication in its urban environment.

Because it was a free and flexible urban community, it was unencumbered by the captivity of institutional paraphernalia. The first decay set in when the church became the custodian of things rather than a communicator of God's message. The early church was not a building on a corner, but a dynamic redemptive people capable of relating indigenously both to the masses in the marketplaces and to persons in family settings within the urban context. This was the dynamism which gave birth to the churches of the New Testament era.

Conflict

Because of its heterogeneous and mobile nature, an urban society is characterized by conflict. This is in contrast to the more homogeneous and static rural society which is characterized by harmony. A rural society is steeped in an agrarian ideology which relates to the cycles of nature and the harmonious order which it seems to foster. Like the ancient Confucian ethic, it conforms to nature rather than endeavors to control it or manage it. An urban society, however, is not nature-oriented, surrendering to its apparently harmonious cycles. Rather it is technology-oriented, geared to the progress of industrial and technological developments and the specializations that follow in the wake of this style. With the vast numbers of people involved, with the complexity of heterogeneity, and with the variety of movement—there is no way to avoid conflict. However, it is out of conflict itself that progress is made. For urban man learns to manage conflict and to carve out of urban complexity not only progress but order. It is a style very much in keeping with the history orientation of the biblical faith. The Bible acknowledges nature—indeed gives it its full due—but its basic orientation is historical. Biblical ideology is not patterned after the cycles of nature, but after the linear movement of the historical process. In this sense an urban society is very much more in the biblical mood than is a rural society. The God of history is the God of the city. For the city increasingly is the habitat of man. The cross-cultural involvements of church growth in an urban world bring identities and ideologies into conflict. The church growth which added Grecian Jews to the former all-Palestinian Jewish church in Jerusalem led to a conflict between these two factors. The first innovation in administration in the Jerusalem Church was designed to manage that conflict. The first interchurch council was called to develop a plan for the management of the ideological conflict which resulted directly from the church growth which brought Gentiles into a previously all-Jewish community of faith.

Secularization

The early church in its simple institutional expression tended to be secular. It had no temple, no priestly elite, no cultus. Its only shrine was the world; its only priesthood, its people; its only worship, the liturgy of praise and involvement. A fellowship of faith, it had no "sacred place," no "sacred days," no "sacred men"—that holy triad out of which all traditional religion had been made. Thus institutionally the New Testament church was indigenous to its secular, urban context.

An adequate theology of urbanism must speak vitally to the phenomenon of secularization. Harvey Cox has made a helpful distinction between secularism as a world view and secularization as a process.[1] We have viewed negatively the idea of secularism, the world view which has no place for God. However, we may view secularization in a positive way, for it refers to the shift in society from the dominant rule of the "sacral" to the dominant rule of the nonsacral. Cox sees this process as having its roots in the Bible itself, especially in the Old Testament events of the creation, the Exodus, and Sinai. This positive interpretation of secularization is in harmony with the prophetic faith of the Old Testament which challenged the sacred establishment. Most of all, it is in harmony with the teachings of Jesus in the New Testament.

Jesus said to the Samaritan woman at the well: "Woman, believe me, the hour is coming when neither on this mountain nor in Jerusalem will you worship the Father. But the hour is coming, and now is, when the true worshipers will worship the Father in spirit and truth, for such the Father seeks to worship him. God is Spirit, and those who worship him must worship him in spirit and in truth" (John 4:21,23–24). In other words, there are no more holy hills. In Christianity under the new covenant there is not a special set of sacred things: places, days, names. There is no special sacred order through which God works. He works in all of life. Such a view of secularization is in harmony with the free church tradition of separation of church and state and the right of man to be free from the rule of a sacred order and free to serve God out of choice and not coercion. We therefore celebrate the process of secularization.

It is indeed this very secularization which frees one from traditional ties and provides him with a new sense of liberty and openness that creates the climate for a free exchange of ideas. This urban openness, largely created by the process of secularization in the New Testament, provided the fertile soil in which New Testament Christianity took roots in the cities of the Graeco-Roman world of the first century. It is understandable why Paul would leave the religious climate of the synagogue in Ephesus and choose the secular climate of the school of Tyrannus as the base for the beginning of the church in Ephesus and the penetration into Asia Minor.

The positive aspect of secularization is well illustrated from the situation in India today. People in the village areas are much more bound to their traditional religion, the caste system, and other dehumanizing characteristics which are inherent in this sacralism. However, upon moving to urban centers, people tend to be liberated from the throes of the caste system and are much more open to new ideologies. In the urban context people are especially open to the message of Christianity. In this view secularization is a liberating process indeed. Secular culture therefore does not rule out God but rather becomes the social context in which true evangelism can thrive, liberated from the shackles of tradition, religious or otherwise.

Secularization therefore has relevance in terms of the biblical background of our faith, especially the New Testament. To cope with modern secularization, the church may benefit greatly from a deeper understanding of the secular roots of the biblical tradition. It is this biblical emphasis which must be applied to our faith as it relates to the modern urban world. Only in this way will the church have its best opportunity to grow and flourish.

Change

As the church in urban society seeks to understand itself in the face of change, it is supported by its own source of authority, the Bible itself. The concept of change relates to the basic theme of the word of God. The definitive act of redemptive revelation in the Old Testament is the Exodus deliverance. It was not only an event that occurred in the context of change, it was an act

which itself created great social change. The Christ event brought
the greatest social change in history. The Bible is at home with
change.

Not only is change a common feature of the objective redemptive work of God in history, change is inevitable in the subjective
response of man to God's redemptive work in history. Conversion
is basic to Christian experience, and conversion is change. Rather
than being threatened by change, the church today should be at
home with change. A truly biblical faith is especially suited for
times of change. Christianity is a crisis faith for a crisis age. One
of the most obvious things we learn from the model of New Testament evangelism is that when people were caught up in the midst
of change, they were most responsive to the message of the gospel.

The greater the change in our time, the greater the spiritual
hunger brought on by the deep vacuum created in the hearts of
people as a result of that great change. Despite massive indifference
and rampant materialism, the new cities of today have brought
the greatest interest in spiritual things we have witnessed in our
time. This attests to one overriding reality. The revolutionary
social change which has accompanied the intensification of urbanization has created a vast spiritual void. With this has come a
unique and challenging opportunity for evangelism and church
growth. It was true in New Testament times. It is true in our
time.

The New Testament church as a spiritual community moved
relevantly in its urban context. It resisted its evil, coped with its
conflict, accepted its paradox, accented its good, seized its opportunities, and grew. It is therefore an excellent model for the urban
church today both in terms of its theological foundation and the
principles of growth which emerged out of that foundation.

Notes

[1] Harvey Cox, *The Secular City* (New York: The Macmillan Co., 1965), pp. 18–
21.

8 Theological Correctives for Healthy Growth

Current theological reflection on church growth must focus on the biblical principles of healthy growth which will serve as correctives for the imbalance found in much of the theory which is popular today. The biblical basis for church growth in terms of traditional theological categories has been well covered in previous studies.[1] What is needed now is a theological examination of the more controversial current church growth theory. The focal point of the controversy over imbalance is best illustrated from the current discussions on the homogeneous unit principle (see Introduction). The concern for a more healthy view has precipitated this controversy.

All growth is not healthy. There are at least four areas in which we are able to see patterns of unhealthy growth. We may illustrate from simple analogies taken from horticulture and medicine. (1) One of these is in the situation where growth is too fast. For example, some plants can grow so rapidly that they fail to bear fruit. This growth is undesirable, though it may be very impressive. There is also the analogy of the human pathology of acromegaly in which the hands, feet, and face of a person grow progressively larger to the point of abnormality. Needless to say such physical growth is very undesirable. (2) Then there is the growth of "suckers." Anyone familiar with raising tomatoes commercially will be aware of this. As the tomatoes grow and are staked, they are also pruned. When extra growth appears around the base of the stalk or between the stalk and the limbs, this growth, which is "sucker growth," is pruned away. The Bible talks about pruning as well as growth. It is a necessary part of the process if there is to be maximum productivity. (3) A third type of unhealthy growth is parasitic growth, a growth that lives and thrives at the expense of another organic entity. We do not have to look far to see that this analogy can be applied to churches. (4) The most serious aspect of unhealthy growth is malignant growth. Cancer is a growth. There is the tendency too often to attach great if not ultimate significance to numerical growth. If a group is enjoying such growth, it is assumed that everything about that group must be all right. Some of the fastest growing religious groups today, however, are the Unification Church, Mormons, Jehovah's Witnesses and others.

The Homogeneous Unit Principle

The ideas inherent in the concept of the "homogeneous unit principle" seem best to reflect the imbalance in current church growth theory. Therefore, the most helpful way to focus on the correctives for a healthy view of growth is to examine this principle and its implications from a theological perspective. Wagner says concerning this principle: "Of all the scientific hypotheses developed within the church growth framework, this one as nearly as any approaches a 'law.' " [2] McGavran calls it "one of the most fruitful concepts to be born in the church growth school of thought." [3] He defines it as "a section of society in which all members have some characteristic in common." [4] Wagner gives a more popular definition: "simply a group of people who consider each other to be 'our kind of people.' " [5]

McGavran makes it clear that he is thinking of this unit in terms of class, caste, race, tribe, clan, or some such clearly defined cultural group. He sees these not simply as units to be evangelized as units and to be formed into churches accordingly—he also sees in "the tribe or caste, the clan or other unit one of God's orders of preservation." [6] Wagner also makes it clear that he is referring to such basic cultural and social categories.

Homogeneous Versus Heterogeneous Principle

Before we look at the theological questions relating to this issue, let us look at the homogeneous unit concept in relation to urbanism. A serious problem in making this principle the normative strategy for church growth is that an urban society is heterogeneous in the normative expression of its public life. It is true that the homogeneous groups exist in the private sphere and are therefore a legitimate expression of urban life. However, a strategy which is geared almost exclusively to homogeneity fails to recognize the significance of heterogeneity in urban society. We have strongly emphasized this as a communication principle to take seriously in a mass society.

Another aspect of urban life that is significant in this regard is change. People are constantly changing in the urban context, moving out of one identity into another and moving as a daily life-style in a cross-cultural and ever-changing social pattern. The public pressures of a massive and complex urban society are enormous. To get on this wave length means we must develop a strategy from the "heterogeneous principle."

Understandable Aspects

There is one way in which this principle may not be objectionable. People are to be affirmed as they are, as persons within their own culturally unique group. Seeing people as they are socially is a way of being aware of the unique needs of special people. No person should be forced to change his culture for another. Minorities are to be commended for their self-determination. "Imperialistic unity" is no unity at all—only uniformity. Pragmatism as such is not objectionable. We have strongly emphasized and shall continue to accent the theological and sociological soundness of the indigenous principle. Churches should develop naturally within their respective cultural contexts. The language problem clearly illustrates the need for certain groups to have the proper homogeneous context for communication in both evangelism and church life. Where there is this need, language churches are not only desirable but necessary.

We can go a step further. Persons and groups have their obvious limitations. Circumstances, resources, cultural and language barriers, and any number of other realities limit how effectively we are able to reach others. It is wise strategy to reach for those with whom we can best communicate or those who best respond to us. This first step can lead beyond and across barriers to those not as easy to relate to and reach. The problem comes when we refuse to evangelize or make welcome in our churches those who, in the language of Wagner, are not "our kind of folks."

We must live with our limitations. Too, we must accept much that is not ideal. The urban style often forces us into a less than ideal pragmation. This is one thing. However, to make this normative, to yield to these limitations, to accent the divisions that separate people, to see them as desirable—that is another thing altogether. To reach an untouchable, one must recognize the reality of "untouchableness"—indeed he may have to rely upon another untouchable to reach him. However, to accept the reality of caste as, in the language of McGavran, "one of God's orders" is theologically unthinkable.

A Positive View of the Minority Church

As we view this whole problem, two important points need to be made about the minority church which is usually strongly homogeneous. Although what we say has universal application, the specific frame of reference is to the United States. The first has to do with the black church. This minority church was created originally out of a survival motivation when blacks were treated as second-class Christians in their own predominantly white churches. Blacks therefore developed their own church with its unique style in spiritual isolation from their white brothers as well as in social isolation from the majority culture. This tragic division was the black Christian's only choice. It has been therefore primarily the black church only which has been able to speak to the black person's need; and because of what the majority culture has created, it has made it extremely difficult for the black church to address the needs of nonblacks. Therefore, we cannot expect the black church suddenly to rectify theologically a problem which it did not create and of which it has been the victim. We live in the presence of this judgment of God upon his church.

A similar situation exists within other minority churches. Although there are significant differences in historical backgrounds, their are parallel problems which persist until today. Minorities—including Christians within the larger church context—often feel isolated from and sometimes threatened by the majority church and society. Therefore, because of a circumstance forced upon them from without, the support of their own ethnic church becomes a means of their spiritual as much as ethnic survival. Again, we live in the presence of this judgment of God upon his church.

Even though we cannot surrender the ideal and ultimate theological premise that every church is sent to everyone, Christian fairness demands that our whole discussion of this subject keep in mind the reality described above. The amazing thing is that today many minority churches are effectively reaching out to those not of their "own kind," and not a few have developed into healthy, growing multiethnic congregations.

The situation of the majority is fundamentally different. Its separation from the minority generally has been one of ostracism by the majority. Supported and protected by the majority system traditionally, it did not in the past necessarily have to be aggressive and obvious in the matter. The reality of this attitude has been woefully evident, however, and it continues today. The concept of "our kind" plays right into the hands of this theological weakness and provides a rationale for an unhealthy church life. Out of it can only come an unhealthy church growth philosophy, especially since such a view is deliberately built upon this principle.

The Crux of the Theological Problem

There is something deeply disturbing about this "our kind" of growth philosophy. It is so foreign to what we see and sense in the New Testament. The emphasis there is upon the mission as "his," upon the church as "his" not "ours." What is more, in human relational terms the emphasis and spirit of the New Testament are upon "his," "hers" and "others" not the self-serving little world of "mine" or "ours."

The very language used by Wagner—"our kind of people"—

makes the homogeneous unit strategy immediately suspect from a theological point of view. He admits that "without doubt, it is the most controversial of all church growth principles." [7] He cites the article in the evangelical magazine *Eternity*, "Where Church Growth Fails the Gospel." [8] Rather than answer the theological arguments presented there, however, Wagner speaks to the controversy from the standpoint of the failure of the American dream of integration and the guilt we have about it. This is skirting the fundamental theological issue. Likewise, when McGavran speaks to the issue from the standpoint of the ecumenical movement, he is not speaking to the basic theological concern surrounding this controversy.[9]

McGavran's definitive maxim is: "men like to become Christians without crossing racial, linguistic, or class barriers." [10] In the first place, no man establishes the terms on which he will receive the gospel—the gospel establishes its own terms. The question is not what one *likes* to do to be saved but what one *must* do to be saved. The crux of the theological problem with this principle is that it operates on the assumption that the strongest ties which bind people are the human ties of culture. In the final analysis it treats evangelism like any other human transaction and the church like any other social organization. We ask the question: Where is the transcendent dimension? In evangelism, where is the convicting work of the Holy Spirit and the change which conversion brings? In the church, where is the unity in diversity which Paul emphasizes? If the boundaries of the church and culture are one, where is the difference that Christ makes? If they are the same, how does one know the difference?

No one denies that this reflects the evangelism and church life which has been the reality in many cases, but do we make this "culture-evangelism" and "culture-church" the norm of our strategy, as this view suggests?

New Testament Correctives

The New Testament recognizes the divisiveness of cultural differences and treats it as a problem: Jew *versus* Gentile, Jew *versus*

Samaritan, Greek *versus* Barbarian, Judaic Hebrew *versus* Hellenistic Hebrew. It makes it clear that the Gospel seeks to unite all men who are so divided. We see this from the historical accounts of the New Testament. The church at Jerusalem was made up of interethnic Jews. Three thousand of these international Jews united with the 120 of the original Christian community on the day of Pentecost. There is no doubt that this early church held regularly many small group meetings, but there is not the slightest hint that they were divided into small ethnic congregations or even ethnic units. In fact, the one thing which is emphasized over and over again is that there was great unity in this church at Jerusalem among these people who were not only from different ethnic backgrounds but from different social and economic classes. An examination of Acts 2:41–47 makes this indisputably clear. Moreover, when the conflict arose over the alleged favoritism shown to Judaic Hebrew widows above Hellenistic Hebrew widows, the solution was not to divide these people according to their ethnic and cultural differences. The solution was to handle the problem administrationally. Thus deacons were selected to give special attention to such matters *that there might be unity in the church.*

As the early chapters of the apostolic church unfold, we find Philip preaching to the Samaritans without any hint of any kind of communication problem between Philip the Jew and the Samaritans. Moreover, when the Spirit of God led Philip to join the Ethiopian eunuch, there was no problem relating to this cross-cultural communication. Later in Acts we find God taking the initiative to teach the apostle Peter a profound lesson growing out of his ethnic self-consciousness and his antiethnic attitude toward non-Jews. Ethics and evangelism were inherently related.

The book of Acts recognizes this difference in cultural reality, but it does not cater to it. In fact, the one thing which is very clear is that the power of God through the gospel eliminates cultural divisiveness. In the church in Antioch of Syria we read of at least two Hellenistic Jews who were from Africa. Therefore, we can assume that the leadership of the church in Antioch was multiethnic, if not multiracial. The Jerusalem Council was convened for the specific purpose of dealing with the problem confronting the church when great numbers of non-Jewish people were becoming Christians. There was not the slightest entertainment of the notion that the church should divide into a Jewish contingency and a Gentile contingency. Rather, there was a bit of ecclesiastical diplomacy and the issue was settled. Unless we define homogeneous in such a way as to make it meaningless, it is clear that the New Testament Church did not grow on the basis of this principle.

When we look at the clear teaching of the New Testament relating to the problem, there should be no doubt about its position, especially that of the apostle Paul. Such passages as Galatians 3:26–28, Colossians 3:11, 1 Corinthians 12:13, Ephesians 2:10–22 should remove all doubt. In fact, salvation is described in the New Testament in terms of the reconciliation of Jews and Gentiles into one body. Both the empirical data (the actual account of what happened in the early church) and the doctrinal ideology (the clear teaching of the New Testament directly on the subject) make a very strong case for the theology of the matter. Admittedly there is the strategic problem as it relates to the use of the homogeneous unit as a methodology. The problem boils down to two opposing realities which have to be dealt with theologically if there is to be a satisfactory answer to the problem strategically. The two opposing facts are on the one hand the value of the homogeneous principle in communication and on the other hand the divisiveness of the cultural conflicts between the homogeneous units in society and the church. The New Testament solves this dilemma by saying that in both doctrine and practice the gospel brings men to a greater unity than their cultural oneness provides, and that is the unity of the Spirit in the body of Christ. The event of Acts 2 and the teaching of Ephesians 2 are definitive in this regard.

When McGavran uses the Scriptures to justify his principle, he ends up (unwittingly) arguing against himself. He says: "Ephesians 2:18 to 3:16 speaks as if Jews and Gentiles, while in 'one single body' continued culturally Jews and Gentiles." [11] This is exactly the point. McGavran seems to think by introducing the idea of "diversity in one body," he is supporting his thesis. But his thesis is to separate the diverse groups, each in its own distinct sphere. To have culturally diverse groups in a single body, of which Paul speaks, is not to have a homogeneous unit but a heterogeneous unit. There is unity, yes, but not cultural unity—rather spiritual unity. However, the one thing McGavran is not arguing for in the homogeneous unit is spiritual unity. In fact, he refers to a culturally diverse church as a "mongrel congregation" [12]— a strange way to designate what Paul calls in effect a spiritual union with cultural diversity.

The New Testament and the homogeneous unit strategy seem in clear opposition both in attitude and practice: (1) Although both the New Testament and this strategy recognize the reality of cultural differences, the homogeneous strategy sees it as desirable, but the New Testament sees it as undesirable. (2) Because it sees it as desirable, the homogeneous unit strategy employs the principle as a definitive strategy of church growth; whereas because the New Testament sees it as undesirable, it shows how the gospel both ideologically and practically destroys its divisiveness. (3) The end result of the homogeneous unit strategy is that it perpetuates not simply in society but within the church itself the divisiveness inherent in the conflict between different cultures. The New Testament, on the other hand, provides a dynamic of unity in the gospel itself and the leadership of the Holy Spirit which is "supracultural" and which destroys divisive human differences and provides a greater unity in the Spirit.

There are at least three theological dangers in the homogeneous unit strategy: (1) it assumes an essentially anthropological rather than theological view of man; (2) it assumes an essentially sociological rather than theological view of the church; (3) it assumes an essentially pragmatic rather than theological view of strategy. It is a kind of Machiavellian form of mission theory where the end justifies the means. Wagner confesses to this, saying that the end is the only thing which justifies the means. [13] That is not the point. The issue is whether the end justifies *any* means, and the theological answer is, "no." It justifies only the means consistent with the nature and spirit of the end.

The Need for Sound Interpretation

This kind of pragmation gets us into trouble Biblically. Wagner's use of Scripture illustrates this. He says that "the homogeneous unit principle should operate in . . . the membership circle and fellowship circle if the church is to grow well." [14] Wagner elaborates: "However, it need not operate in what I would like to call the 'citizenship' circle, referring to citizenship in the kingdom of God. It is on this level that Christians need to demonstrate the walls of partition have in fact been destroyed in Jesus Christ." [15] This is a classic example of biblical rationalization and illustrates the need for sound biblical exegesis in church growth theology. For Paul declares clearly that it is in the fellowship of the body of Christ, the church, that the middle wall is broken down (Eph. 2). This is precisely Paul's language, and his meaning is indisputably clear. We have no right to pick the bits of biblical language and concepts which suit us and make them fit into our schemes. Rather we are first compelled to determine the clear teaching of Scripture and then to develop our schemes from there. Wagner confesses shame that we have done so poorly in removing the wall of partition within the citizenship circle and suggests that perhaps the reason is "we have not thoroughly understood the homogeneous unit principle." [16] The truth of the matter is that if the walls of partition are not destroyed at the level of church fellowship, as Paul's theology demands, they are not likely to be destroyed at the level of kingdom citizenship.

Questionable Means—Questionable End

In the whole line of argument about "means" and "end," there is a question about what the true Christian end is. Church growth is natural, normative, and deeply desirable, but it is not the theological ultimate. That is the glory of God. The planting of *any* kind ("our kind") of churches (class, culture, racist, etc.) by *any* means (proselyting, church splits, appeal to rural nostalgia or even to racism)—all of which has and is being done—is hardly the type of thing which glorifies God. Is church growth so hard up as to need this kind of rationale and motivation?

This kind of appeal to popular "successism" by *any* means to *questionable* ends is not the kind of motivation we need for healthy growth. We *must* have a sounder theological base. Sometimes in human eyes the will of God is to fail and even to die. Stephen is a good example. Our Lord himself is the classic example.

We realize, of course, that those who advocate this philosophy do not wish these negative dimensions. Their writings otherwise make this clear. However, when they develop such concepts, especially when they phrase them the way they do, they can only excite this kind of theological concern.

A Way Out for the Homogeneous Unit Principle

McGavran says: "The church . . . always grows in homogeneous units." [17] Wagner says: "Show me a growing church, and I will show you a homogeneous unit. There may be exceptions to the rule, but I have not found one yet." [18] This is incredible. Such churches do exist by the thousands. Moreover, some of them are even growing phenomenally. Because these growing churches obviously do not fit the concept, at times they stretch the philosophy to include most anything, the whole Methodist Church of India, for example.[19] Wagner even uses the concept of "psychological" to so classify an otherwise nonhomogeneous group like the Circle Free Church of Chicago.[20] This is confusing, to say the least. This use of the principle is so broad, it makes it essentially worthless as a frame of reference. How can we take both interpretations seriously?

This latter view, which virtually destroys the concept as defined earlier, would pose little problem if any to those who are otherwise disturbed by the concept. In fact, in this latter understanding, churches could reflect the very kind of health which we hope to see in church growth. Fuller trained Tom Wolf, pastor of the

First Southern Baptist Church, Los Angeles, feels that his church has grown by this method (this inspiring story is told in chap. 10). He calls his church a MOAB 2. By this he means that it is made up of Mexicans, Orientals, Anglos, and blacks who are at phase 2 in their cultural pilgrimage: neither strictly ethnic nor totally Americanized. If this is a homogeneous unit, power to it. We suspect, however, knowing this church, that this is only one of a number of factors supporting the more basic spiritual fellowship which is the strongest unifying force of the church. Other supporting factors would be strong pastoral leadership, lay involvement, and community identification. The above healthy picture is a far cry from the connotations of caste as "God's order" and "our kind of people."

Death by the Homogeneous Unit

If the homogeneous unit principle is responsible for growth—it is also responsible for death. Selective evangelism which has built the "our kind" of churches has been one of our greatest problems. It is these very class and culture churches which have died because they could not change and be the church in a changing and changed community. This once successful "homogeneous evangelism" and these once growing "homogeneous churches" are now in deep trouble.

Do we want church growth at any cost? By settling for pragmatic expediency where we can see fast growth quick without taking cognizance of the kind of growth it is or the kinds of problems that might eventuate from this particular pattern of growth, we are in theological trouble. Also, if we think only of growth and do not come to terms with other issues which may be as important and even more ultimate than growth, we are again in theological trouble. Moreover, if we pursue this course, we might very well be putting ourselves in the position of pursuing a strategy which enables us to win many battles but in reality places us in a basically vulnerable position where we are virtually guaranteed that we shall lose the war. When this happens, we are in both theological and strategic trouble.

Life and Health Through Balanced Growth

The Bible presents a balanced picture of growth. We read of Jesus that he increased in wisdom and in stature and in favor with God and man (Luke 2:52). It is said of John the Baptist that "the child grew and became strong in spirit" (Luke 1:80), and of Jesus that "the child grew and became strong, filled with wisdom" (Luke 2:40). The references here are to physical, mental, and spiritual growth. The New Testament places a strong emphasis upon total growth. Peter speaks of growing in grace and in the knowledge of Christ (2 Pet. 3:18). Paul speaks of our increasing in the fruit of righteousness (2 Cor. 9:10). He also speaks of growing in faith (2 Thess. 1:3). In the thinking of Paul, the ultimate aim of the Christian life is to grow "to mature manhood, to the measure of the stature of the fullness of Christ" (Eph. 4:13). The church growth described in the book of Acts (as we carefully observed in chap. 3) is in harmony with this general concept of total and balanced growth which is found in the New Testament at large.

A healthy theology of church growth therefore must build upon this biblical view of balance and total growth. There should be influential growth as well as organic growth, spiritual growth as well as numerical growth, multiplication growth as well as enlargement growth. Moreover, all growth itself must balance with all other aspects of Christian teaching and practice. Only when the total Christian expression is in balance can there be life and health.

Notes

[1] Robert Calvin Guy, "Theological Foundations," *Church Growth and Christian Mission;* Arthur Glasser, "Church Growth and Theology," *God, Man, and Church Growth,* "Church Growth Theology," *Church Growth Movement;* Harvie M. Conn, "God's Plan for Church Growth: An Overview," *Theological Perspectives on Church Growth;* A. R. Tippett, *Church Growth and the Word of God* (see Bibliography).

[2] C. Peter Wagner, *Your Church Can Grow,* p. 110.

[3] Donald McGavran, "The Homogeneous Unit in Mission Theory," *Church*

Growth Movement (Proceedings Eleventh Biennial Meeting Association of Professors of Missions) Nashville, Tenn., June 12–14, 1972, p. 46.

4 Ibid.

5 Wagner, Op. cit.

6 Op. cit., p. 56.

7 Wagner, p. 111.

8 Rufus Jones, "Where Church Growth Fails the Gospel," *Eternity*. June, 1975.

9 McGavran, p. 53.

10 McGavran, *Understanding Church Growth* (Grand Rapids: William B. Eerdmans Publishing Company, 1970), p. 198.

11 McGavran, "The Homogeneous Unit in Church Growth Theory," p. 54.

12 Ibid., p. 5.

13 Wagner, p. 137.

14 Ibid., pp. 121–22.

15 Ibid., p. 122.

16 Ibid.

17 McGavran, p. 47.

18 McGavran, p. 47.

19 Wagner, p. 116.

20 Wagner, p. 117.

PART IV

Strategy: How Churches *Can* Grow

9 A Comprehensive Approach to Strategy

A comprehensive approach to strategy is built upon the healthy balanced view of urban church growth accented in the previous chapter. It is concerned with total growth: influential as well as organic, qualitative as well as numerical, multiplication as well as enlargement. Also part of this strategy of total growth is the focus upon growth in the transitional areas as well as the more promising areas out on the growing edges of the megalopolis. Therefore, the two concluding chapters will deal respectively with these divergent dimensions of the modern city.

Cooperation Within the Larger Christian Community

There has been a growing interest in church growth by both denominational and parachurch groups. These religious communities have much to offer each other. It would be extremely helpful if some kind of cooperative structure with broad guidelines could be established for the sharing of resources at all possible levels.

Research

In order to avoid needless duplication of personnel, time, and energy and in order for each group to have the advantage of the total resources available, the creation of an interchurch clearing house for church growth studies and special research would be invaluable. The William Carey Library, closely connected with Fuller, has filled a vital need in this direction. Two urgent needs exist today: (1) the sharing of existing materials on the part of denominational research departments, college and seminary libraries, research-oriented parachurch groups, and others; (2) the projection of needed studies where there might be either a division

of labor or the pooling of expertise, as the case may demand. Out of this could come a regularly published printout of all available materials in the field. Such a service, available to all in this cooperative endeavor, would readily reveal two valuable items: what is available and what needs to be done. An example of the potential in this regard is seen in the significant work which has already been done by such excellent research groups as MARC and the Missionary Research Library.

Training

A part of the above available data would be current information on what is being offered regularly in church growth in the various schools. This would provide information on schools which specialize in certain areas such as urban church growth. It would also provide information on special courses for limited times. As a part of such a cooperative arrangement, schools could work together in providing or hosting special conferences dealing with special areas of concern in the church growth field. Also, there could be opportunities for dialogue sessions in which certain controversial areas could be discussed with a view to a better understanding.

Pilot Programs

Another exciting possibility would be for such a group to sponsor a pilot program in a key urban area. This pooling of funds, personnel, time, and expertise for a given period with adequate follow-up and evaluation could prove to be of great value. Of course, there would have to be mutually acceptable guidelines, and such a program would need to be projected with great care. It may prove that such an effort could best be done on an individual denominational basis, leaving the above suggested cooperative endeavor limited to research and special training. However, such a pilot program would be worth at least one effort. It would be worth the expenditure of persons, funds, and time for the lessons it would teach, and it could offer local areas a cooperative model to follow on their own initiative in a given urban area, if they should so choose.

A Denomination's Thrust

Church growth is the normal concern of a denomination, and a number of agencies have especially strong commitments to it. For example, in the Southern Baptist Convention, both the Foreign Mission Board and the Home Mission Board have church extension as a concern of high priority. The Sunday School Board also emphasizes church growth with a strong focus on enlargement growth. State conventions and associations, nearer to the churches, have church enlargement and multiplication as prime concerns. However, church growth in all of its facets should concern every entity of church and denominational life. We have tried to emphasize strongly that a healthy church growth is a balanced one. It is dependent upon all of church life for its support and for the most meaningful context in which it projects itself. At the same time, the rest of church life is dependent upon church growth for its institutional survival, although this should never be its motivation for church growth. In addition to the usual intradenominational concerns for church growth, the Southern Baptist Convention has adopted an overall program for the rest of this century: "Bold Mission Thrust." It is a daring plan to present every person in the world with an opportunity to receive the gospel by the year 2000. The home goal is to provide a Christian church within walking distance of every person in America. No "thrust" could focus more clearly on the need for church growth.

A Bold Plan to Use Students

We shall deal in the final chapter with a model of a denominational strategy in a given urban area. We turn now to consider one fascinating prospect in church growth opportunity. It concerns an extensive plan to use students as an integrative strategy of urban church extension.

For the last few years the Department of Church Extension of the Home Mission Board has cooperated with the six Southern Baptist seminaries and the state conventions in an exciting approach to beginning new work. It is the "Church Extension Sum-

mer Seminar." The Board pays each student a weekly stipend plus his expenses to and from the field. The state convention and local association pay all the local expenses of the student. The student spends ten weeks on a field working with another team member (which may be a spouse), helping to start a new work. The student works under local church sponsorship and a local supervisor who oversees his work and meets weekly with him in an evaluative session.

Before the students leave for the field, they are a part of a three-day intensive orientation session at the seminary. The orientation team is composed of the professor, Home Mission Board specialists, and the local supervisors. The students are selected earlier in the year and are given a list of ten books to read before and during the experience. They are trained and supervised in a number of skills: surveying, personal witnessing, Backyard Bible Clubs, putting on a public "event" such as a gospel concert, and conducting a Home Fellowship Bible Class. The professor makes a visit to the field for one day's evaluation session with each team. The goal is to start a new work, however humble.

The student keeps a daily log and gives an in-depth evaluation of his experience at the end of the summer. Upon completion of the full requirements, the student receives six hours of credit. A three-day intensive orientation is held each fall under Board sponsorship for the benefit of the professors and local supervisors who work with the students. Last summer's experience is evaluated and plans are made for the next summer. In 1977 there were 87 students in the program. In 1978 there were 162 students. So far, the average permanent new work started through this program has been one for every two teams.

Why not make this a year-round program? True, it would require a greater investment of personnel, time, and money on the part of all concerned: Home Mission Board, seminary, state convention, association. But what could be worth more? There are 12,000 ministerial students in Southern Baptist colleges (not counting several thousand in other colleges). With 9,000 current seminary students and the rich prospects for the near future, the student resources are enormous. If the program demanded it, college students could be used. For a number of years the Calvary-Arrowhead Baptist Association has successfully used California Baptist College students in church extension in the Riverside area. The seminaries could develop a significant intern concept as a part of this program. Too, they could accelerate their development of extension centers and provide a widespread base for the program.

Look at the benefits of such a venture: (1) As a part of a comprehensive strategy it would provide an unprecedented opportunity for intradenominational cooperation. (2) It would provide a seminary intern model par excellence. (3) It would provide the best possible context for learning how to start new work, the field itself. (4) It would provide the field with a committed company of additional laborers (young, energetic, optimistic). (5) It would ensure that new work would receive the priority which it deserves. (6) It would provide professors and local specialists (supervisors) with new exposures and opportunities to enhance their understanding of church extension. (7) It would force all parties concerned into an alertness in order to ensure that the student has a valid project and that the local situation has a good opportunity to produce a new work. (8) It would provide us in time with a wealth of experience and understanding at many levels in the field of church extension. (9) It would provide us with the churches we need in order to reach and minister to our emerging urban world. (10) It would ensure that these thousands of young people presently preparing for the ministry will have churches to pastor— for at our present rate, they certainly will not. (11) It would provide the student with both a field-oriented education and an expertise in church extension which would be immeasurable as a credential for the ministry. Of course, the student would balance this with the rest of his seminary studies, and a curriculum would be designed to make it a part of a learning experience in which all the components are well integrated and properly related. By what other means could we provide in one program such an investment both in new work and in the ministry of tomorrow—and significantly a ministry trained in church growth *in the field?*

What Is the Ideal Church?

Important to our consideration is the question of what size and type of church is most ideal for the general health of an urban church growth strategy? A comprehensive approach would suggest a variety of sizes and types. And this is exactly what the urban context has produced. Let us look critically at sizes and types.

The Ideal Size

There are built-in advantages and disadvantages to any size church, and there are exceptions (sometimes notable) to any generalizations which are made about them. The *large church* has these basic advantages: (1) it is a "megachurch" in a "megasociety," a part of urban massiveness; (2) it has a strong visibility in the urban landscape; (3) it offers its families an impressive variety of services; (4) it has the resources to make an impact in the city; (5) it can afford to give up people and funds for new work. Its basic disadvantages are: (1) it tends to be too impersonal; (2) there tends to be a small percentage of membership involvement; (3) there is usually a smaller percentage of baptisms than in a small church; (4) there is the tendency to spoil people (which does not make for servanthood and a sense of mission); (5) some today may resent its imposing edifice.

The *small church* usually has these basic advantages: (1) a family atmosphere with a strong sense of belonging; (2) closeness to the local community; (3) a high percentage of membership participation and baptisms. Its disadvantages are: (1) little variety of services to its families; (2) overworked leadership; (3) tendency toward nonprogressiveness; (4) little impact on the city as a whole; (5) difficulty in giving up people to begin new work.

The *medium-sized church* tends to have the best of both worlds. It tends to be strong enough to overcome the usual objections to the small church and small enough to overcome those of the large church. It may, however, get caught in the middle and not be quite large enough to provide what people expect in a large church and not quite small enough to provide what is expected in a small church. Regardless of how the above falls, one real plus is that it is strong enough to give up people for new work. The conclusion is that in the variety of urban life there seems to be room—perhaps even necessity—for the different sizes of churches it has produced.

The Ideal Style

There will be no effort here to sit in judgment upon any particular style of church as such, though we feel the necessity to point up strengths and weaknesses. It is quite clear that urban geography has produced a type of church for every aspect of that geography: downtown, uptown, inner city, ethnic ghetto, neighborhood, suburb, and so on. Most of these congregations emerged indigenously to meet the numerous and varied spiritual needs of urban man.

We have observed earlier the tendency of urban institutions to reflect the three basic attitudes toward urban life within the city: the positive, the adaptive, and the negative. As a general rule we would suggest that the more positive a church is about its urban context the more healthy it will be. Although the adaptive mentality refers to a greater identification with the primary group experience adapted to urban life from the village past, it is not usually antiurban. Churches which find themselves reflecting this attitude, however, need to strive toward a greater identification with the larger urban reality. Churches with a more negative urban mentality need to examine their motivation. If it is a basic antiurban pattern, there will result a basic ineffectiveness in the urban context. The church will become ghettoized. If, however, it is a reaction to the evil of which the city is capable, it may be justified. For example, the storefront is basically a reaction church, but its reaction may be against the depersonalization of the city, and therefore it may be well positioned to serve effectively its area of social deprivation. Though some church types seem more susceptible to certain attitudes than others, most any type can reflect any of the three categories.

There are advantages and disadvantages in both traditional and innovative styles. The more traditional church has such advantages as church building visibility and aesthetic appeal, but it tends to be building-bound and suffers from this edifice complex which can prevent creativity. Such a church finds itself most vulnerable to urban social change. A basic type of innovation is the use of rented facilities. They have the advantage of quickness, flexibility, relative inexpensiveness, and attraction by people who will not go to a church edifice. They have the disadvantages of little aesthetic appeal, lack of permanence, and limited facilities. The storefront, which may be owned or rented, has the above advantages and disadvantages. Its greatest asset is its friendliness, but it does carry a stigma. There are some people who would never identify with it.

The Ideal Style for Church Growth

Of all the styles of church life, there is one which seems to offer the best possibilities for growth. If it can overcome its tendency to be completely self-centered, the base-satellite church, using the house church model of satellite, seems to be the most promising. We shall discuss more fully the problems and prospects of this model in the final chapter. However, a few points are significant at this juncture. The advantages of this model are as follows: (1) most any church can develop this style; (2) it offers a balance of impact (through the base) and penetration (through the home meetings); (3) it offers in one model the advantages of the larger church (base) and the smaller church (satellite); (4) it satisfies the more traditional desires (base) and the more innovative (satellite); (5) with its mobile and more secular expressions, it is indigenous to urban life. It is an international model which is proving to be one of the fastest and most effective means of church growth.

"Doing It Right"

In our urban world of rapid change, we must have a sense of urgency and expectancy about church growth. The traditional conservative approaches are too slow. The greatest heresy in church growth theology is that smokescreen of a statement: "We're going to wait until we can do it right." By this is meant that we wait until we have enough money to buy property and build a first unit and have enough people to fill it. If this is our strategy (nonstrategy!), while we are waiting the megalopolis with its rapid movement will run over us and with its massiveness will bury us. If we have a hundred families with which to start new work, the best method would be not to start one strong work but ten or perhaps twenty immediately, and in homes. Churches are not started with money, they are started with people. Money can buy a lot of things including people. But it cannot buy the kind of people needed to start new churches. Given the right kind of people, under the direction of the Holy Spirit, money can buy a lot of aids in the work of church extension. And this is significant.

We need to start just as the early Christians started under the impetus of the Holy Spirit. For their mass meetings they used what was available. For their small groups, they met in homes. When it became desirable they rented a facility (Paul at Ephesus). This is the basic pattern for us today. Beyond this churches ought to develop naturally in their various settings to meet the needs which are there. The gospel sits in judgment upon all types—even the most indigenously urban, the most theologically sound, the most strategically healthy.

10 The Inner City: Renewal and New Growth

There can be no adequate urban church growth strategy that does not address itself seriously to the reversal of the declining trends in the transitional inner city. We have observed the drastic need for renewal of the inner city church. It is now time to look seriously at reasons for the decline and the principles of renewal which can reverse the trend and spark new growth in these declining churches.

Reasons for Decline

Cultural and Class Identity

If this crisis has taught us anything, it is that our churches often have a more pronounced cultural or class identity than a theological one. This is not an effort to sit in judgment on any given congregation, but the overwhelming evidence is that many congregations have faced a serious crisis when their communities changed because they could not relate to the new people surrounding the church after the neighborhood had changed. They either refused to do so, or they did not know how. In places where this has been true, the only alternative the congregation has had was to move or die. When this happens, it seems obvious that the church's deepest identity is a cultural or class one. It may use all the expected religious language, but its most ultimate decisions are made not on the basis of theological identity but cultural or class identity. Its first self-image, whatever else it deems itself to be, is that of a congregation designed to serve a certain class of people or to follow a certain cultural tradition. In some cases its cultural captivity has been tragically apparent.

Theological Weakness

The heart of this problem is theological. In the final analysis it proves that the church has not seen itself as servant, as a community of faith, as a missionary fellowship—despite the lip service it may give to these theological understandings of the church. When a congregation consciously shuts out anybody because of racial identity, economic status, or any other reason based upon class or social values, it reveals a fundamental theological void. Even the churches which admit that the gospel is for all and that the church should reach out to all—if they do not do it consciously, reflect the same theological weakness.

Lack of a Sense of Mission

Related to this theological weakness—indeed a part of it—is a church's complete preoccupation with itself. Its decisions are always made on the basis of institutional self-interest. It is survival-oriented, not ministry-oriented. Studies have shown that these churches are usually the quickest to capitulate. The apostolic church crossed the greatest possible barriers: from the Jewish to the Gentile world, from the Eastern to the Western world. This brought great threats but the church was on mission—possessed of a burning passion to share the faith—and therefore took these revolutionary changes in stride. The inability of our churches to cope with radical social change is indicative of how far removed we are from the caliber of church life which characterized the apostolic community.

Complex Barriers Between People

In all fairness, however, it must be said that not all transitional churches have declined because of cultural captivity, theological weakness, or lack of sense of mission. Some have declined because of the cultural barriers which face different groups. Some churches have actually tried to reach out to all, but have been hindered by differences in culture, language, economics, and other social reasons. Churches are made up of people who, despite their dedication and openness, have honest limitations. A church may honestly try, but it may be unable to change adequately or quickly enough to avoid a crisis. Moreover, in some multiethnic settings, where the various ethnic identities are unusually strong, to appeal to one is to alienate the other. What is a church to do in this regard?

The religious cultural differences can be just as divisive. There are sometimes significant differences between persons of the same faith but of different racial backgrounds. Black and white Baptists, for example, are often separated by obvious theological, ecclesiastical, liturgical, missiological, and administrational differences.

Another profound dimension is psychological. For example, once doors which have been previously closed are open to blacks, they cannot be expected suddenly to rush in and become instant members of communities which earlier had totally rejected them. Often suspicions have to be overcome. Moreover, many times there is discomfort in relating to new ideas, new styles, and new settings which do not have the protection of one's traditional cultural and religious environment and way of life.

Economics

Then there is the pragmatic problem of economics. Indeed, some feel that this is really the whole problem. Churches cannot maintain their staffs and facilities with the decreased resources of a nonmiddle-class membership. However, this is never a problem of simple economics. A church is not bound either to the church facility or the staff. If it is, its problem is not simply an economic one. Churches that refuse to adapt to the social realities about them are only asking for a crisis. In the meantime, however, the bills have to be paid. The church has to make a decision about its building—whether to rent part of it, to share it, to sell all or part of it and move to a different style of ministry. If the staff has to go, how does the church handle it? These are questions which relate to economics. The point is that a church does not have to decline in its ministry to people, even in the number of people it is reaching, when it changes its style of worship and outreach to be more indigenous to its new social context. In many cases, a change has meant not only renewal but new growth.

Reversing the Trend

When the impact of the urban exit reached the sensitivities of the larger Christian community, there was positive response. Many of the urban church studies of the sixties were theological responses to this massive default in the central city. Theologians and churchmen alike spoke candidly to the problem, and urban mission strategists and pastors responded in concrete counteraction. The result has been an encouraging development in the life of the urban church. Though some churches continue to move and die, there is a new mood and a new trend in the transitional communities of the country. Single congregations on their own and others with denominational help (often not financial), have faced their cultural captivity and have dealt with it theologically. The result has been a fresh sense of apostolic mission and in many cases a completely renewed style of church life. Dozens of books have been written, especially over the last two decades, to tell these inspiring stories of triumph in the central city. Let us examine some of these inspiring stories, using as examples a number of Southern Baptist churches in California.

The First Southern Baptist Church of San Jose, California which also goes by the same name in Spanish, is located at the edge of the inner city in the rundown area of the old business district of San Jose. When Jerry DeOliveira went to the church as pastor in 1970 there were forty active members, twenty-five of whom were Mexicans-Americans from Del Rio, Texas. Today, the church averages around 200 in Sunday School attendance. It is a multiethnic church with eight different Latin American countries represented. Counting all of the Latin nations as one, there are eight different ethnic backgrounds represented in the membership: Spanish-speaking, Portuguese-speaking, Italian, Japanese, Lithuanian, blacks, Anglos, etc. Sixty percent of the members are Latin American. There is a Japanese associate pastor. The church conducts each Sunday two services in English and one service in Spanish, which is translated into English. DeOliveira has a deep commitment to reach all people in his congregation and has paid a severe price personally to resist the temptation on the part of the original members to keep it not only as a Spanish-speaking church but as a Mexican-American church.[1]

The First Southern Baptist Church of Compton in the Los Angeles area is located in a racially changing community. From 1965 to 1970 the population changed from 5 percent black to 75 percent black. At the end of this period, the church declined from approximately 200 to 100. Sidney Smith, a Southern Baptist home missionary working in Christian social ministries in the Los Angeles area, was invited by the white pastor to locate his offices in the church facilities. By the time the white pastor had resigned, the attendance had dwindled to some thirty people, 95 percent of whom were white. At this time Sidney Smith was invited to serve as interim pastor. He was able to lead the church to a completely open door policy. A black Southern Baptist pastor was invited to the church. Now the attendance is consistently around 150. Reflecting the essential community makeup, 90 percent of the members are black and 10 percent are white.[2]

The Central Baptist Church of Inglewood, California is also in a community which has witnessed a rapid change in ethnic structure. In 1971 the community around the church, which is the Crenshaw-Imperial area of Los Angeles, was 30 percent black. In 1973 it was 50 percent black. In 1975 it was 75 percent black. In 1977 it was between 80 to 85 percent black. Earlier, before the community changed so drastically, the church was predominantly white and had some 200 members. However, in 1973 when the white pastor left, the attendance was down to 14 whites and 3 blacks, the total active membership. In 1974 a retired superintendent of missions, Harry Lichty, Sr., came to the church to lead the church in a strategy to reach the community which was now predominantly black. Early in 1975 Luther Keith was invited to the church as an associate. Lichty trained Keith to become permanent pastor. Late in 1975 Lichty stepped out, and Keith became the full-time senior pastor of the church. In the first seven months of his ministry the church baptized 89 people. In the first year and a half in which Keith was pastor of the church, there were some 300 additions. The church now averages around 250 in consistent attendance. The church is indigenous to its community, the membership reflecting almost exactly the ethnic population makeup of its community.[3]

The First Southern Baptist Church of Los Angeles is located in an integrated community which began changing some twenty years ago and is now beginning to experience a second change. The first change was from predominantly white to black and Spanish-speaking. The next change which is taking place now is being brought about by the movement into the area of a large number of Asians. When Tom Wolf became pastor of the church around 1970, the church had been in decline and was averaging around 90 in attendance. Now the church averages over 400. The average attendance for January through March, 1977 was 411. The average for April, 1977 was 460. For the year of 1976 the church increased its A.M. worship service 64 percent. The church Sunday School attendance increased 53 percent in 1976. The average evening worship service is 220 with 190 in Church Training. When Tom Wolf came to the church there were two Mexican families in the congregation. Today the ethnic makeup of the church is as follows: 60 percent Mexican-American, 30 percent Anglo, 10 percent blacks, Asians, and other ethnic minorities. Some 70 percent of the Sunday School staff is single. The church has a Mexican-American associate pastor. A film has been made on the church entitled *They Said It Couldn't Be Done.* Last year this church was close to the top in the state both in number of baptisms and percentage of baptisms.[4]

Achieving Balanced Growth

One striking thing about these transitional inner city churches is the fact that they not only have experienced numerical growth in their racially changing settings, they have also grown as multiethnic congregations. Also it is evident that these churches have been growing qualitatively and influentially as they have been growing quantitatively. In fact, their numerical growth seems definitely a result of the fact that there have been other kinds of

growth. In other words, the growth in these churches has been very balanced growth, not simply numerical growth. Churches in transitional areas need to be very aware of their capability to grow in this manner. Often when there is a numerical decline, pastors and churches reach for some kind of gimmick which is designed primarily to increase statistical growth. However, the best way to achieve numerical growth in transitional areas is to develop the kind of well-rounded and balanced church life and program which provides the spiritual basis for total growth.

The Need for a Support System

One of the highest priorities for denominations as they address the problem of church decline in transitional areas is the development of a support system. This system must be spiritual and moral as well as material. First of all, there should be a special awareness of the critical need of our inner city churches. This awareness should be matched with a concern which is clearly communicated. There should be opportunities for pastors in transitional situations to receive counsel to deal with personal psychological needs growing out of the trauma of transition. In addition there should be structured group meetings in which pastors who share common problems in the inner city can draw strength from each other. Also the strength of a denomination's work in any given urban center should be marshaled to the support, spiritually and materially, of pastors and their people who are experiencing crises in their church situations. Some progress is being made in this regard.

In addition to spiritual and moral support, there needs to be a structured concern. There should be concrete plans for research to determine the nature, extent, and timing of the transitional situations. Where possible there should be financial resources within the denomination from which hurting situations can draw as a part of a strategy of renewal. Even when financial resources are not available, however, ways must be found to assist pastor and people in hurting transitional situations. This is one of our highest priorities. It is as important to conserve what we have as it is to develop new work. What shall be our net increase i

we grow impressively in the outer city but collapse at the core?

It should not be implied, however, that the only place to plan for new work is in new areas. A comprehensive strategy should plan for completely new work in the spiritually disenfranchised areas which have been abandoned by traditional churches. In recent years, Southern Baptists have developed effective new work programs in transitional areas in such major urban areas as Houston, Detroit, Greater Los Angeles, and the San Francisco Bay area. These new congregations usually reflect in their membership composition the essential ethnic makeup of their respective areas.

Notes

[1] Taped interview of Jerry DeOliveira by Sidney Smith; personal interview with DeOliveira.
[2] Personal interview with Sidney Smith.
[3] Personal interview with Luther Keith.
[4] Personal interview with Tom Wolf.

11 The Growing Edge: Advance on All Fronts

We come now to consider a model for church growth based upon the need for church extension or multiplication growth. The enlargement of single congregations is vital to the total concern for church growth, but this falls far short of the kind of growth we read about in Acts and the kind of growth we need in order to keep up with the megalopolis.

The Must of Multiplication

We are awed by the megachurches, and they play an important role. However, there is the need for as great a diffusion of congregations as possible. One large church, no matter how excellent its outreach is, is limited in what it is able to do unless it mothers other churches which in turn can mother others. The megachurches have learned that the best way to grow is to create new units. Consequently, some have developed the base-satellite method. Southern Baptists learned many years ago that an excellent way to grow a church is through the Sunday School. Moreover, the secret of the enlargement of the Sunday School, and consequently the church, is the creation of new units—more and more classes. The Independent Baptists borrowed this "Sunday School method" and with it have built some of the largest churches in America. The problem with this method is that it has tended to be only enlargement growth. The new units only made the single church larger. The megachurches with the satellite method followed the same principle but added to it the principle of diffusion by creating semicongregational units outside the structure of the mother base. This added a modified multiplication principle to the enlargement principle. As effective as this model is, it has one significant weakness. Because of a system which keeps the satellite bound to the base, the satellite is never free to become a base itself with a capacity to multiply. The base-satellite mega-church has a built-in self-centeredness.

Contrasting Models: Jerusalem and Antioch

There are two basic models of growth in Acts: Jerusalem and Antioch. Jerusalem was a megachurch with at least 10,000 members very early in its life. Although it did reach out to Samaria, most of its growth was in Jerusalem. It had many home meetings, the ancient equivalent of the modern satellite. Despite its incredible growth and mammoth size, however, it could not mother the historic mission movement of the faith. The reason was it was never quite able to give itself away. The less prestigious, smaller Antioch church, on the other hand, had that power to release itself. It was therefore the chosen instrument for that far-reaching ministry. The Jerusalem church enjoyed enlargement growth; the Antioch church, multiplication growth—not for itself but for the Kingdom. Jerusalem was the center of orthodoxy; Antioch of mission. The Jerusalem church possessed the authority of "the Word"; the Antioch church, the authority of "the presence." In Jerusalem was "the apostolate of tradition"; in Antioch, "the apos-tolate of function." The apostleship of the twelve in Jerusalem was one of "office." The apostleship of Paul and Barnabas was one of "mission." Both traditions are a part of our tradition, and we need both today. Indeed Antioch built upon Jerusalem. But Jerusalem alone is not adequate. It is the Antiochian tradition which provides us with the ultimate model of church growth. Jerusalem kept the faith—Antioch passed it on. Ephesus moved in the Antiochian tradition and both enlarged and multiplied itself.

The Parable of the Banyan Tree

We therefore look to the beginning of new work if Christianity is to grow and flourish. There is a parable in the banyan tree. This unique tree grows by its branches dropping new shoots into the ground which in turn take root. The tree therefore becomes an intricate web of branches and trunks. Each new trunk develops branches which in turn drop more shoots into the ground to become new trunks. This chain reaction produces an ever-widening entity covering in time acres of ground. The largest banyan tree is in Sri Lanka (formerly Ceylon), and one of the largest is in the botanical gardens of Calcutta, India. Despite this tree's capacity to become the largest in circumference in the world, because it is a single entity, it is limited in how far it can reach. Likewise, the giant base-satellite church, though the largest in the world, because it is a single entity—with its satellites bound to it like a new trunk in a banyan tree—is limited in how far it can reach. Even with the use of all the forms of urban communication— the mass public meeting, the printed page, radio, and TV—which the superchurches use quite well, there is still a limit.

There is another side of the banyan tree story. It also produces seed. It therefore has the power to reproduce itself almost without limit. In its ability to give itself away—to free part of itself to become a banyan tree in its own right—it has its most far-reaching effect. So it is with a church. Let a church like a banyan tree grow as large as it can, but let it at the same time share part of itself for the growth of the Kingdom.

The Base of Operation

We learn from Jerusalem, Antioch, and Ephesus that there must be a base of operation if there is to be effective growth. We especially observe from Acts the importance of Antioch and Ephesus as bases from which patterns of growth emerged in regions beyond. Because the work was so new in the apostolic period and there was only one church in each city, the base had to be a single congregation. Today, however, the base can be one created out of a committed community of cooperative churches. A denomination must have such a structure in every major urban area if it is to be effective in the growth of new churches. Baptists have a natural in this regard in the association, an organization of cooperative churches usually serving the county area of a metropolitan center.

This base is first of all a people-base, as it was in Antioch and Ephesus. In Ephesus there was a meeting place, and sometimes a building is desirable. Indeed the association has its office, and it has its meeting places. The operation, however, is a people operation. The association is an "idea" around which people rally in the cause of church outreach.

The base is also a spiritual base. As was true of Jerusalem, Antioch, and Ephesus, it is the *point* where the people of God catch the missionary vision and dedicate themselves to the task. It is the *occasion* where dreams are dreamed and plans are made. It is the *time* of commissioning. It is *where* and *when* and *how* and *why* God moves on his people, as he moves them out on mission to grow his churches.

The Primacy of Leadership

An effective urban church growth strategy needs leadership, at least one church growth specialist and preferably a staff to furnish leadership in the several supportive and related functions of a city mission program. In the Baptist association, the chief administrative leader, usually known as the director of missions, should be a church growth specialist or should have such a specialist on his staff. The same should be true with any denomination. We have found that the best channel through which to project new work is the Associational Missions Committee. This committee under the direction of the urban church growth specialist spearheads the new work outreach of the association.

From all the studies which have been made on church growth, nothing is more obvious than the necessity for leadership. Often the vision of one single leader can turn the tide of a declining church situation. The dream of one man can build a spiritual empire in a decade or two. Small groups of leaders have changed the course of history. From Peter and Paul to the present, this has been the case.

Cooperative Commitment of Churches

The existing churches in the city must be the Antiochs and

Ephesuses of today. This will come only out of a spiritual impetus and an unselfish desire to start new churches. The commitment to a program of church growth through new work by a community of cooperating churches is the most important single prerequisite for the effectiveness of such a program. The commitment of the pastors and church leaders of these cooperating churches is crucial. Only they can inspire the involvement of people from their churches in new work projects.

Every church, no matter how small, can be involved in some way. The stronger churches have a special stewardship in this regard. There are at least three basic reasons why a church should be involved in new work: (1) it is right and Christian to share God given strengths and resources, (2) it places the church in the apostolic tradition of doing God's work, (3) it brings enrich-ment and spiritual blessing.

There are four areas in which a church can assist in beginning a new work. (1) The most important is to provide a nucleus of people, preferably of persons who live in an area where a new church is needed. (2) The next most important thing is to provide persons who will assist in surveys, personal evangelism, and other needed ministries. A special need is a faithful nucleus which will stay with a project until enough new people are reached to begin a work. (3) Prayer and moral support are valuable contributions. (4) As much as it is needed, money is perhaps the least important item. Money at the right time and in the right place is crucial, but without committed people and spiritual and moral backing it is next to worthless in a local church new work ministry.

Elements of an Urban Strategy

Urban church growth theory must be tested in the crucible of an actual urban setting. Moreover, if a strategy is to be effective, it must be projected on the basis of a manageable urban region. The geography of the typical Baptist city association, usually encompassing the larger metropolitan region, is ideal. It is large enough to reflect all of the normal and varied expressions of an urban region. Yet it is not so large that it is unmanageable.

Benefitting from the general research in the field and the expertise growing out of it, the local urban region becomes the testing ground for a denomination's effectiveness in urban church planting. Knowledge of principles applied through the dedicated leadership and cooperative labors of a community of committed churches constitutes the dynamic of effective church planting. What a city-wide church extension strategy is able to plan and project through the combined strength of the churches, it is able to implement through the sponsorship of individual churches. Yet the churches can be so much more effective in beginning new work because of this background strength and cooperative undergirding.

Survey the Territory

The first step in an effective urban church planting strategy is to survey the territory. Careful attention should be given to the church needs of every area of the megalopolis: downtown and uptown, the transitional inner city, the slum, the ghetto, the university and other specialized communities, the suburbs and the exurbs, the urban-rural fringe, the new urban-oriented resort centers in rural areas. Special care should be exercised in understanding any significant changes which are in the offing for the area.

There should be a thorough understanding of growth plans and projection for the larger urban area and its region. Paralleling this should be plans for a new work in each emerging new area. Part of this aspect should be plans to purchase property in strategic areas of promise for future church sites.

Urban church planters should be aware of the latest information from the city and regional planning offices. There is usually a wealth of general information about cities from this and related sources in the city.

Building on this general information, special surveys should be conducted of the newer communities in the suburbs and exurbs, on the rural-urban fringes, and in the new rurban areas. The telephone survey can be used to gain a maximum amount of information, in a brief period, with a minimum of effort. People can be used in this form of survey who can not serve in a door to door survey.

The door to door survey is the best if enough people can be enlisted. There is no substitute for a personal contact with persons. In February of 1978, the San Francisco Peninsula Southern Baptist Association sponsored a week-long survey where persons from its cooperating churches came each night and on Saturday to visit a new churchless area to enroll persons in a Bible study. The plan from the beginning was to start a new church in the area. The combined strength of the churches was able in a week to enlist enough people for the nucleus of a new work in an area where Baptists are not strong. The experience was electrifying for the church visitors, and the project brought new enthusiasm to the association.

Determine Priority Areas

Since it is impossible to go in every direction at once, priorities should be established on the basis of the data provided by the survey: (1) the most unchurched areas, (2) the most responsive areas, (3) the most strategically influential areas. Through the establishment of priorities, effort can be concentrated on the most advisable locations with the maximum use of resources and the best stewardship of means. When priority areas are established, churches should be enlisted as sponsors, with the best backing possible from the resources of the larger community of congregations.

Enlist and Train Workers

The next step is to enlist and train workers. There are basically two kinds of workers which are needed in a strong program of church planting: (1) those who will work at the level of impact, and (2) those who will work at the level of penetration. The former group is deployed primarily in setting the stage in a given area in preparation for the work of a sponsoring church which will actually develop the new work. The latter group may be a general group, working as a part of the larger urban strategy team and moving from one area to another as the situation demands. In some cases, and perhaps in most cases, these penetration teams are a part of the local congregation which is sponsoring the new work. They may be especially selected and trained either to help start the new work or to be a permanent nucleus out of which the new church will develop. In addition to these especially equipped persons, people from the churches can be rallied for special one-night or one-week operations for survey, personal evangelism, and other essentials in preparation for new work. In this case, persons who already have expertise will volunteer or can be trained without lengthy sessions.

Impact the Target Area

We have seen from the beginning of this study the necessity for impact if communication is to take place in an urban context Therefore, the principle of impact must be a vital part of an urban church growth strategy. An area can be impacted in a number of ways. It must come in some form of mass communication.

1. Radio and television make the greatest impact. The association or its equivalent can best see that an area is impacted through mass media. As good as individual church efforts are in this regard, they accrue primarily to the benefit of that single congregation (and we acknowledge all the good which is done in this way). What is needed, however, is the use of cooperative resources to be directed in such a way as to use radio and television for cultivating areas where new work is needed. Of course, the single congregation can use this effective medium for beginning new work, if it will. However, it should be more than an effort to multiply its own captive satellites (remember the parable of the banyan tree). If the strong churches would use their access to the media for starting new work with the purpose from the beginning of developing autonomous congregations, they could render an invaluable service to the kingdom. Even when they do, however, they should work as a part of a larger strategy—both to contribute to and benefit from that strategy. Moreover, an adequate strategy

must use the electronic media as a basic point of operation apart from what individual churches are able to do in this regard. The biggest problem, of course, is the expense. However, there are ways to overcome some of the high cost through the development of expertise in the knowledge and use of this communication process.

2. Literature makes a significant impact. Newspaper ads, and, better still, feature stories in the daily newspaper (or perhaps the special weekly paper of the area) are very effective. Even brochures and tracts, if they are attractively done and if they are widely distributed in a brief block of time, will make an impact. This ancient form of urban communication is still a fundamental medium, but it needs to be contemporary and indigenous if it is to be effective.

3. Mass meetings, as we have observed from earlier chapters, are as important as ever in the modern urban era. There are basically two styles: the general and the localized. The former is designed to reach as much of a general area as possible, and the latter zeros in on a given community or subcommunity. Such meetings may take the form of an evangelistic campaign or rally. However, they may take the form of some other "event" such as a musical, a drama, or a movie. Church musical groups have been especially effective in providing concerts as a part of "impacting" an area in preparation for new work. When there may not be funds for radio, television, and newspaper ads, these type of "events" are available, and they are effective.

Penetrate the Community

Impact must be balanced with penetration in the urban setting, as we have repeatedly observed in this study. Communication is not complete until it does. Personal and small group communication is necessary for penetration. In a careful strategy, this can begin with a survey. This is the beginning of the personal contact. The next step is personal witnessing as a follow-up on the survey information. Cultivative evangelism should precede more aggressive styles. Evangelism is necessary, and persons should be trained in both personal and group evangelism. Persons should be trained in how to make an evangelistic call, how to cultivate, and how to lead persons and families to Christ.

They should also be trained in how to lead a small group along the line of friendship and fellowship evangelism. Persons should be trained in how to apply a Bible lesson evangelistically, and how to study a contemporary problem from a biblical perspective and how to apply the principles evangelistically.

Other types of small group penetrations are important. Backyard Bible Clubs, sidewalk dramas, neighborhood puppet shows, and other such events make some impact in the community as well as open up homes for cultivation evangelism. What can be done in given areas depends on the area. What needs to be done depends upon the nature of the community. In some cases, some type of service such as a medical clinic, mobile or stationary, may be the first penetration of the Christian witness in a neighborhood.

Commit the New Work Leadership

We have heavily accented the crucial importance of leadership. A new work will rise or fall at the point of the leadership which guides it in its formative stages. Potential leadership for new work can be found among three significant groups of ministers: (1) bivocational pastors, (2) lay "shepherds," (3) ministerial students. The bivocational pastor has played a significant role in church planting and development. Thousands of churches have been founded and/or nurtured by these committed servants of God over the years and over the world. This company of ministers constitutes a resource par excellence for new work. We have observed from the study of such churches as the Yoido Island Church in Seoul, Korea, the almost incredible potential of the lay "shepherd" for church leadership. It has the greatest potential of any type of leadership in a new work strategy. Churches all over the world should learn from this inspiring model of leadership. We have already illustrated the significant contribution college and seminary ministerial students can make in providing the leadership needed for this work (see chap. 9).

We have a rich source indeed from which to draw in providing leadership for new work. What is needed is commitment to this type of work. It is an exceedingly rewarding calling, and it will require a level of dedication equal to any type of church ministry. It is wise before we begin the first stages of planning—or as soon thereafter as possible—to have a leader totally committed to this new work.

Decide on the Meeting Place

There are a number of places where new work can be started. Some of the most common are: (1) homes, (2) schools, (3) storefronts, (4) community halls. The latter three are rented facilities and have advantages and disadvantages (see chap. 9). However, thousands of churches have been started in them, and in some cases, especially the store buildings, they have made good permanent homes for some congregations, as we have observed earlier.

The home has been the most common beginning place for churches from the apostolic period until today, and it is increasingly becoming a more permanent type of church home. The use of the home has many advantages: (1) it is a natural setting for the household of God; (2) it is a biblical method; (3) it is an urban method; (4) it is the most economical way to begin a new work; (5) it is flexible; (6) some people will go to a home when they will not go to a church edifice; (7) it is an international method; (8) it appeals to all classes of people; (9) it lends itself to a surprising variety of styles. Some form of the "house church" can be found among all types and classes of Christian groups all over the world.

There are some disadvantages to home meetings: (1) limitation of space; (2) complaints from neighbors; (3) problem of what to do with children; (4) some people prefer a traditional church facility for religious service; (5) the informal setting is vulnerable to religious proselytes and cranks. In most cases, however, these do not pose serious problems; and for the purpose usually served by home meetings, the above problems can be managed.

The proliferation of home meetings in recent years has resulted in a number of distinct styles of the "house church." They may be classified in several categories in terms of their relation to other churches: (1) the satellite, (2) the federated, (3) the independent. The satellite house group may be temporary or permanent. It is a smaller unit of a larger mother unit to which it is subsidiary. The federated house group is a fellowship of house congregations relatively equal in size without a larger mother base in the sense of a strong, traditional church in a traditional facility with a permanent geographic base. The fellowship of house groups may rent a facility for a combined weekly service. The independent house group may or may not in some way relate to other house groups or traditional church groups, but there is no structural tie to them. It may even be a denominational church, but it is autonomous and relates to the denomination as would any other congregation.

The "house church" has come to be a general term used to describe a wide variety of styles in home meetings. In terms of style, there are three basic categories: (1) the home fellowship, (2) the Christian house, (3) the house congregation. The home fellowship may be a Bible study group, a fellowship-discussion group, a prayer group, or any variety of related groups. It may be a satellite of a mother church large or small, permanent or temporary. It may be an arm of the church or the beginning of a new work designed to become an autonomous church. It may be an essentially unrelated group drawing from one or more churches, sometimes across denominational lines. It may also draw religious seekers not previously church connected. These unrelated groups may or may not be in competition with churches. In some cases, however, they are viewed in this way by the churches. The Christian house is a home where Christians live more or less communally. It functions as both a home and a church. In recent years these houses have come to serve as a church for others in addition to the residents: friends, former residents, neighbors, etc. The house congregation is a community of Christians which meets in a home, usually of one of its members. It is an autonomous church, denominational or unaffiliated, though it may have some members who also have other regular church ties. It may meet on Sunday or some other day. Its distinctiveness is that it functions as a church, not a fellowship, and it is not a subsidiary of another church. Of the three, the first two are by far the most common.

The above picture of the "house church" indicates its vast potential for church extension. It should be a firm lesson to us to take advantage of this economic, flexible, and natural means of beginning new work. House groups have come about both spontaneously and as planned units. The home fellowship has been both spontaneous and planned, with the satellite the best example of the latter. The Christian houses have been primarily a spontaneous Christian expression of the counterculture communes that came into prominence in the sixties. Once they emerged, some planning for new Christian houses has resulted from a kind of strategy. There is no reason why all of these extremely functional urban house types can not be a part of a master strategy for our urban age.

Plan for a Good Beginning

The beginning of a new work is crucial. No detail should be left to whim, though ample room should be allowed for the development of spontaneity. If the proper leader is committed, and the beginning nucleus is dedicated to the cause, the other matters usually will fall in place. Although the details of meeting place, time, arrangements, curriculum, literature, and such matters need to be attended to with careful stewardship, the mechanics of the process should fit into the larger spiritual dimensions. A prayerful attitude, Christian love and friendliness, reliance upon the Holy Spirit, a strong emphasis upon the Scriptures, and sensitivity to the needs of the people and community should characterize the beginnings.

A Local Church Model for New Work

We have seen how crucial and significant the role of the local church is in an effective urban church growth strategy. We turn now to look at the actual implementation of a new work plan by a local church. We shall assume a normative situation: a medium size church with limited but adequate resources both to contribute to the general strategy of the local urban region of which it is a part, and to be a responsible and aggressive sponsor of its own new work outreach as the cutting edge expression of that general strategy.

Create a Climate for Growth

The pastor and church leaders should actively work at sensitizing the people to the need of the church to be unselfishly involved in new work. Preaching, teaching, seminars, audiovisuals, and every available source should be employed to this end. Bible studies, prayer sessions, and sharing groups will accent the Christian truths about loving, caring, and reaching out in ministry and evangelism. Emphasis should be placed upon the joys of mothering a new congregation. This mood should be established as a permanent aspect of church life.

Establish a Church Missions Committee

The church then should concretize this sensitivity by creating its own local missions committee to work closely with the Associational Missions Committee. This committee will guide the church through its new work pilgrimage. This committee will enlist a nucleus of dedicated people who will serve in two basic capacities: (1) part of an associational team to serve in special areas as the needs may arise; (2) a task force of lay leadership in beginning a new work under the sponsorship of its own church. The former might be persons gifted in the arts (music, drama) and other special areas, and the latter will be those gifted in ministry, evangelism, and small group work. This group may either be the nucleus of a new work or help reach new people who will form that nucleus.

Train Workers for New Work Ministry

The next step is to train workers. This should be the kind of training which sensitizes workers to the needs of people and how to minister to them. There should be training in the usual skills such as surveying, personal evangelism, and how to conduct a Home Fellowship Bible class. In addition to persons whom the church will train, it can make meaningful use of bivocational ministers, lay "shepherds," and students from the larger urban church community.

Select the Area for New Work

As a result of research by the missions committee in cooperation with associational missions committee, an area should be selected. Surveys should be designed to determine people's total needs as well as their immediate responsiveness to the gospel. Every effort should be made to relate to the community as meaningfully as possible, to minister to the total needs of persons.

Begin a Home Fellowship Bible Study

The most ideal method is to begin an informal Bible Study in the home of a dedicated member of the sponsoring church. If this is not possible, then an effort should be made as soon as possible to secure a home in the community for such a beginning. Persons contacted in the community are invited to the weekly Bible Study. As the group grows through evangelism, new Bible groups should be formed.

Develop Some Form of the House Church

Out of the home Bible studies, the sponsoring church can begin to develop strong house churches. They will develop as satellites of the sponsoring church, but in this case there will be the clear intention for at least some of them to develop into autonomous churches. The house church can either be a permanent type of new work or the first step in the direction of another type.

Use a Cooperative Base-satellite Model

An excellent way for a church to enlarge its own ministry and at the same time have a significant part in new work is through an unselfish approach to the base-satellite method. It is a demon-

strated method of growth, but it needs to work both ways. Its
advantages are obvious, and its potential is almost without limit.
Through this approach churches can also reach out to those who
will never be reached by traditional church methods. Churches
of almost any size can use this method effectively and are doing
so today.

Cooperate in Ongoing Plans

As the church cooperates with the local denominational program in this new work effort, it both contributes to and benefits
from that cooperation. The most healthy approach is for a church
never to move unilaterally but always to work cooperatively. It
is only through churches that we can grow new churches. A denomination may have the best of methods, but without people
from the churches, there will be no new work. For churches are
started, not with methods, but with people. At the same time,
in our complex urban world, the vision of one church, no matter
how encompassing, cannot see all the needs. However, by linking
hands and carefully surveying the field together, all the needs
can be discovered. Cooperation at the surveying, planning, training, and implementing levels will insure maximum results. With
such an approach, we have everything to gain. It will be the
best stewardship of persons, time, money, and expertise. It should
be the most fruitful approach for the kingdom. It will draw us
closer together. It will keep us close to what is close to the heart
of God.

Conclusion
Summary of Principles

The principles of healthy urban church growth have been obvious throughout this study. However, it should be helpful in conclusion to single out most of the significant ones by way of review and summary.

The First Principle: the Spiritual Base. There is no substitute for an adequate spiritual foundation for growth. This is fundamental, and without it all other principles are in vain.

The Theological Principle. The method is inherent in the message. Evangelism grows out of the evangel. Pragmatism, though an urban characteristic, is under the judgment of the gospel. All methods, no matter how effective, are judged by the standards of biblical principles.

The Holy Spirit Principle. Church growth is supremely the work of God. Healthy growth is the work of God's Spirit. We cannot reduce to a science that which is fundamentally the work of the Holy Spirit.

The Leadership Principle. From every source of understanding behind the reason for growth, one thing always emerges as significant—leadership. Next to the spiritual resources themselves, no principle is more important.

The People Principle. God's method is a man, that is, God works through people. Churches are started, not primarily with methods or money, but with dedicated people. Too, effective church growth is person-centered, not program-centered. Effective programs can emerge only as there are people gifted to develop them and people who need them. People must never be mere statistical abstractions.

The Balance Principle. Healthy growth is balanced growth: organic and influential, quantitative and qualitative, enlargement and multiplication. To grow up "in him" is the basis of all true Christian growth.

The Principle of Impact-Penetration Balance. In an urban society mass communication is needed for impact, and small group communication is needed for penetration. These are complementary and are therefore needed in balance for both mass and personal needs of urban man.

The Principle of Presence-Proclamation Balance. The incarnational witness of a healing presence balanced by the proclamation of God's message was the method of Jesus and the early church. Evangelism borne on the wings of ministry is the first step of church growth.

The Rhythm Principle. In the early church both the inward dimensions of worship and fellowship and the outward dimensions of evangelism and ministry were evident. As it grew, the church assembled and dispersed and reassembled and dispersed again in a rhythmic pattern of inward-outward balance.

The Heterogeneous Principle. In an urban society where heterogeneity is the social pattern of public life, the church must be on the same wave length with these massive and complex dimensions if there is to be effective and lasting growth.

The Homogeneous Unit Principle. Because homogeneity is the pattern of primary groups within the city, the homogeneous unit principle has value, but it should always be balanced with the heterogeneous principle. It should never be used primarily as a manipulative pragmatic principle.

The Indigenous Principle. Churches should grow as nearly as possible in a way which is natural, normative, and nonalien to their general and local urban context.

The Principle of Flexibility. In keeping with the urban patterns of mobility and change, church growth methods should always be flexible. Openness to the Holy Spirit's leadership demands it.

The Point of Contact Principle. "Bridging" is not as easy in the urban context as it is in the rural context, but it is necessary if people are to be reached. The best "points" in the city are those that relate to the deepest felt needs of urban man.

The Principle of Responsiveness. This is our view of "God's open door." It is wise stewardship to reach first for those who are most responsive, as long as we are not selective on the basis of wrong Christian motives.

The Principle of Simplicity. It is always wise to "keep it simple." Urban complexity is like trouble. We do not have to borrow any. Enough of it will come soon enough. The best method is as little method as possible.

The Scientific Principle. It is wise to use all of God's gifts. The research and social sciences are especially helpful. Paul is the classic example of "one who had done his research"—he knew his field. Basic to this principle, however, is that all disciplines serve as the handmaidens of Christian theology.

The Cooperative Principle. Cooperation at every level is needed: the local church, the denomination, the larger Christian community. Unselfish desire for kingdom growth is the fundamental attitude which makes it all work.

The Principle of Timing. It is humbling but wise to recognize that we can only work in harmony with God's timetable. Everything else can be right, but if the time is wrong it will not work. If the time is right the most imperfect of components seem to fall in place.

The Love Principle. Agape love is the "law" of urban church growth, if there is a law. Whether it is in the larger heterogeneous setting of urban anonymity or the smaller homogeneous setting of primary groups, *agape* love will win its way to hearts and homes—to people, the beautiful stuff out of which church growth is made.

Bibliography

Urbanism and the Urban Church

ALLEN, DONALD R. *Barefoot in the Church: Sensing the Authentic Through the House Church.* Richmond: John Knox Press, 1973.

ALLEN, ROLAND. *Missionary Methods, St. Paul's or Ours.* Chicago: Moody Press, 1959.

BAKER, THELMA S. *The Urbanization of Man: A Social Science Perspective.* Berkeley: McCutchen Publishing Co., 1972.

COLE, WILLIAM E. *Urban Sociology.* Boston: Houghton Mifflin Co., 1958.

COMMANDER, R. G. *The Story of Union Baptist Association, 1840–1976.* Houston: D. Armstrong Publishers, 1977.

COX, HARVEY. "Mission in a World of Cities," *International Review of Missions* (July, 1966), 273.

_____. *The Secular City.* New York: The Macmillan Co., 1965.

DAVIS, KINGSLEY. "The Urbanization of the Human Population," *Scientific American* (Sept., 1965), 41–63.

DRIGGERS, B. CARLISLE. *The Church in the Changing Community: Crisis or Opportunity.* Atlanta: Home Mission Board of the Southern Baptist Convention, 1977.

ELLUL, JACQUES. *The Meaning of the City.* Grand Rapids: William B. Eerdmans Publishing Co., 1970.

GREENWAY, ROGER S. *An Urban Strategy for Latin America.* Grand Rapids: Baker Book House, 1973.

_____, ed. *Guidelines for Urban Church Planting.* Grand Rapids: Baker Book House, 1976.

JACKSON, DOUGLAS. *The Downtown Church.* Philadelphia: Department of City Work, Division of National Missions of the Methodist Church, 1958.

LEE, ROBERT. *Stranger in the Land: A Study of the Church in Japan.* London: Lutterworth Press, 1967.

LEIFFER, MURRAY H. *Five Residential Churches.* Phil.: Department of City Work, Division of National Missions of the Methodist Church, 1958.

_____. *The Effective City Church.* New York: Abingdon Press, 1961.

MABRY, DON F. *A Study of Churches in Communities in Crisis in Metropolitan Associations in the Southern Baptist Convention, 1973.* Atlanta: Home Mission Board of the Southern Baptist Convention, 1974.

NELSON, JAMES W. *The Rural-Urban Church on the Metropolitan Fringe.* Atlanta: Home Mission Board of the Southern Baptist Convention, 1977.

SCHALLER, LYLE E. *Planning for Protestantism in Urban America.* New York: Abingdon Press, 1965.

SIMMEL, GEORG. "The Metropolis and Mental Life." *The Sociology of Georg Simmel.* Trans. by Kurt Wolff. Glenco: The Free Press, 1950, 409–17.

SMITH, FRED. *Man and His Urban Environment.* New York: Man and His Urban Environment Project, 1972.

Urban Evangelism Strategy Basic Training Manual. Singapore: Singapore Baptist Convention, 1977.

WILSON, ROBERT L. *Methodism in the Inner City.* Philadelphia: Department of City Work, Division of National Missions of the Methodist Church, 1958.

WIRTH, LOUIS. "Urbanism As a Way of Life," *The American Journal of Sociology* (July, 1938), 10–18.

Church Growth

ALLEN, JOHN A. *Associational Missions Committee Church Extension Manual.* Atlanta: Home Mission Board of the Southern Baptist Convention.

BELEW, M. WENDELL. *Churches and How They Grow.* Nashville: Broadman Press, 1971.

BENJAMIN, PAUL. *The Growing Congregation.* Lincoln, Ill: Lincoln Christian College Press, 1972.

CONN, HARVIE M., ed. *Theological Perspectives on Church Growth.* Nutley, N. J.: Presbyterian and Reformed Publishing Co., 1976.

COSTAS, ORLANDO E. *The Church and Its Mission: A Shattering*

Critique from the Third World. Wheaton, Ill.: Tyndale House Publishers, Inc. 1974.

CHANEY, CHARLES L., AND LEWIS, RON S. *Design for Church Growth,* Nashville: Broadman Press, 1977.

GERBER, VIRGIL. "A New Tool for Winning the City," *Church Growth Bulletin* (July, 1976), 542–44.

———. *God's Way to Keep a Church Going and Growing.* Glendale, Ca.: A Division of G/L Publications, 1973.

GLASSER, ARTHUR F. "Church Growth Theology," *Church Growth Movement.* Proceedings Eleventh Biennial Meeting Association of Professors of Missions, 1972.

GREEN, HOLLIS L. *Why Churches Die.* Minneapolis: Bethany Fellowship, 1972.

GUY, ROBERT CALVIN. "Theological Foundations." *Church Growth and Christian Mission.* Ed. Donald McGavran. New York: Harper and Row, Publishers, 1965, 40–56.

HODGES, MELVIN L. *A Guide to Church Planting.* Chicago: Moody Press, 1973.

HUDNUT, ROBERT K. *Church Growth Is Not the Point.* New York: Harper and Row, Publishers, 1975.

KELLEY, DEAN M. *Why Conservative Churches Are Growing.* New York: Harper and Row, Publishers, 1972.

JONES, EZRA EARL. *Strategies for New Churches.* New York: Harper and Row, Publishers, 1976.

JONES, RUFUS. "Where Church Growth Fails the Gospel," *Eternity* (June, 1975.).

McGAVRAN, DONALD, ed. *Crucial Issues in Missions Tomorrow.* Chicago: Moody Press, 1972.

———, ed. *Eye of the Storm: The Great Debate in Mission.* Waco: Word Books, Publishers, 1972.

———. *How Churches Grow.* London: World Dominion Press, 1959.

———. *Understanding Church Growth.* Grand Rapids: William B. Eerdmans Publishing Co., 1970.

———. "The Homogeneous Unit in Mission Theory," *Church Growth Movement.* Proceedings Eleventh Biennial Meeting Association of Professors of Missions, 1972.

McGAVRAN, DONALD, AND ARN, WIN. *How to Grow a Church.* Glendale, Ca.: A Division of G/L Publications, 1975.

McGAVRAN, DONALD A., AND WELD, WAYNE. *Principles of Church Growth.* So. Pasadena, Ca.: William Carey Library, 1971.

PALMER, BERNARD AND MARGORIE. *How Churches Grow.* Minneapolis: Bethany Fellowship, Inc. 1976.

SCHALLER, LYLE E. *Hey, That's Our Church.* New York: Abingdon Press, 1975.

SKELTON, EUGENE. *Ten Fastest Growing Southern Baptist Sunday Schools.* Nashville: Broadman Press, 1974.

STETZ, JOHN. "Biggest Little Church in the World." *Church Growth Bulletin* (September, 1976), 78–83.

TIPPETT, ALAN R., ed. *Church Growth and the Word of God.* Grand Rapids: William B. Eerdmans Publishing Co., 1970.

———. *God, Man and Church Growth.* Grand Rapids: William B. Eerdmans Publishing Co., 1973.

WAGNER, C. PETER. *Frontiers in Missionary Strategy.* Chicago: Moody Press, 1971.

———. *Your Church Can Grow.* Glendale, Ca.: A Division of G/L Publications, 1976.

WERNING, WALDO J. *Vision and Strategy for Church Growth.* Chicago: Moody Press, 1977.

YAMAMORI, TETSUNEO, AND LAWSON, E. LeROY. *Introducing Church Growth.* Cincinnati: A Division of Standard Publishing, 1975.

Index

Abraham 107, 109
African churches 87
Agape love 112, 113, 171
Agri-cities 36
Allen, Roland 46, 47
Anonymity 13, 34, 112–115
Athens 22, 47, 53
Anthropology 14, 129
Anti-city 27
Antioch of Syria, church of 45, 50, 53, 127, 154
Atlanta 78

Babylon 22, 49, 101, 103, 104
Baptist Temple, Houston 73, 94
Balance principle 169, 170
Balanced growth 13–16, 121, 133
Baptist association 156–159
Baptists 58, 67, 148
Base of operation 155–158
Base-satellite church 88, 143, 153, 154, 167, 168
Banyan tree 154, 155
Bivocational pastors 162, 167
Black church 61, 68, 81, 82
Book, the 37, 38
Brazil for Christ Church, Sao Paulo 87, 88

Cain 101–103
Calvary Chapel, Costa Mesa 86
Castors Grace Church, Bangui, Central African Republic 87
Cathedral 59, 61, 62, 79

Central Baptist Church, Inglewood, California 149, 150
Central business district (downtown) 26, 61–63, 142
Change, social 13, 119, 120
Chicago 91, 93, 131
Church Extension Department, Home Mission Board, SBC 138, 139
Church of the Open Door, Marin 89
Church structure 54–56, 72
Circle Free Church, Chicago 131
Cities of refuge 104, 105, 109
City
    ancient 35, 36
    as communication 31
    as extension of man 107–110
    circular 25
    cluster 25
    definition of 32
    industrial 37
    paradox of 97, 107
    Renaissance 22, 37, 58
    strip 25
    technological 39
Comic, the 38, 39
Congregational (church) types 58–69, 76–93
Conflict 13, 34, 116, 117
Cooperation 136–140, 156, 157, 167, 168, 171
Costas, Orlando 14, 15
Cox, Harvey 21, 109

Cultural and class identity 122–126, 132, 145

Decentralization 25, 34
Denominational strategy 138–140, 151, 152, 155–165
Detroit 19, 68, 91, 93
Divisiveness 129, 146, 147
Downtown church (Old First) 59–66, 73, 74, 79, 94

East Harlem Protestant Parish 91
Ecumenical church 90, 91
Eden 107–109
Electronic media 39, 40
Ellul, Jacques 102–105, 108, 109
Enlargement growth 16, 133, 153
Enlisting workers 159
Ephesus and church of 47, 48, 53–55, 119, 154, 155
Ethnic church 59, 61, 68, 80, 81, 94
Ethnic ghetto 142
Evangelism 44–46, 50, 52–54, 56, 114, 139, 161, 162
Events 139, 161
Ex-rural church 92, 94
Exurban church 90
Exurbs, exurbia 26, 27, 90

Federated church 88, 89
First Baptist Church, Hammond, Indiana 86
First Baptist Church, Houston 72, 73, 86, 94
First Baptist Church, Pasadena, Texas 95
First Baptist Church, San Antonio 96
First Southern Baptist Church, Compton, California 149
First Southern Baptist Church, Los Angeles, 131, 132, 150

First Southern Baptist Church, San Jose, California 148, 149
Flexibility, 51, 170
Foreign Mission Board, SBC 138
Fuller Theological Seminary Institute of Church Growth 11, 14–16, 17

Garden Grove Community Church 85–87
Geographic extension 53
Greenway, Roger 11

Healing 43, 48, 71, 162
Healthy growth 121, 133, 136
Heterogeneity 13, 32, 33, 62, 115, 123
Heterogeneous principle 122, 123, 170
Holistic view of growth 14
Holy Spirit 50, 55, 96, 126, 144, 165
Holy Spirit principle 169
Home Fellowship Bible Class 139, 159, 162, 164, 167
Home Mission Board, SBC 78, 138, 139
Homogeneity 33, 34, 123
Homogeneous groups 33, 123
Homogeneous unit principle 16, 122–132, 170
House church 54–56, 59, 82, 83, 163–165, 167
Houston Southern Baptist churches 73, 74, 93–97

Ideal size church 141, 142
Ideal style church 142, 143
Impact-penetration balance principle 40, 115, 170
Impact principle 45, 160, 161
Indigenity 44, 50–52, 114, 142, 144
Indigenous principle 170

Industrial revolution 22, 37, 70
Influential growth 16, 133
Inner city 17–19, 142
Inner-city church 18–19, 60, 61, 77–79, 95–97

Japanese urban church types 60
Jerusalem, church of 22, 43–45, 49, 52, 102, 106–108, 154
Jesus 43, 44, 50, 55, 112–114, 118, 133
Jesus movement 88
Jones, Ezra Earl 12, 75

Jotabeche Methodist Pentecostal Church, Santiago, Chile 87, 88

Kinds of growth 16, 52–54, 132, 133, 136

Language church 61, 80, 81, 123
Large church 141
Large neighborhood church 66
Lausanne 16
Lay shepherds 87, 162, 167
Leadership 156, 159, 160, 162, 163, 166, 167
Leadership principle 169
Lee, Robert 60
Life-style church 92, 93

Malignant growth 122
Mass 31, 34
    communication 29, 32, 35, 36, 39, 40, 44, 160, 161
    evangelism 44, 45, 144, 161
    man 40
    public meeting 35, 36, 47, 48, 161
    relations 40
    society 31, 32
Massive, massiveness 13, 33, 112, 123
Means of growth 50, 71, 96, 97

Medium-sized church 67, 141
Megachurch 85, 86, 87, 153, 154
Megalopolis 23–28, 95
Melodyland Christian Center 86
Metropolis 22, 23, 59
Methodists 60, 68, 131
Meeting places 163–165
Means and end 130, 131
Minority church 124, 125
Mission 45, 46, 109, 146
Missions committee 156, 166
Mobility 13, 33, 35, 45, 62, 115, 116
Money 144, 147, 148
Movie, the 39, 40, 161
Multiple stimuli 33, 34
Multicongregational church 89
Multiethnic church 89, 90
Multiplication growth 16, 133, 136, 153, 154

McGavran, Donald 11–16, 122–124, 126, 128, 129, 131

Neopolis 22
Neighborhood (residential) church 61, 66, 67, 73, 74
New Jerusalem 107
Newspaper, the 38, 40, 161
Nineteenth Avenue Baptist Church, San Francisco 89
Numerical growth 15, 52, 53, 122, 132, 133

Organic growth 16, 133, 136

Parachurch groups 72, 136
Parasitic growth 121, 122
Paul 45–50, 52–56, 128, 130, 133, 144, 154
Penetration principle 47, 159, 161, 162
Pentecost 44, 52, 127

Pentecostals 67, 70, 72
People principle 144, 157, 169
People's church 64, 65, 74
Peoples Temple, San Francisco 86, 87
Periodical, the 38, 40
Peter 44, 112, 127, 133
Philip 45, 52, 112, 127
Pilot programs 137
Place, social importance of 35, 76
Polis 22, 35
Point-of-contact principle 170
Pragmatism 15, 34, 76, 123, 170
Presence-proclamation balance principle 170
Primary relations 31, 34, 35, 40
Printed page (literature) 37–40, 161
Priority areas 159, 167

Qualitative growth 15, 16, 53, 54, 136
Quantitative growth 15, 16, 52, 53, 121

Radio, the 39, 40, 97, 160
Regional church 76, 84
Relocated church 91
Research 136, 137, 158
Responsiveness 124, 159, 167, 171
Rhythm principle 54, 170
Rome 22, 37, 48, 104, 108
Rural, ruralism 23, 24, 31, 33, 34, 35, 111
Rural church in an urban world 92
Rural-urban fringe, church on 84, 85
Rural-urban contrasts 34, 35
Rurban, rurbia 23, 24, 26, 27, 90
Rurban church 90

Samaria 45, 52, 127
San Francisco 68, 86, 89, 93

Schaller, Lyle 12, 75, 76, 92
Scientific principle 136, 137, 171
Second Baptist Church, Houston 73, 94
Second Baptist Church, Little Rock 88
Secondary relations 33, 34
Secularization, secularism 13, 34, 117–119
Seminary intern strategy 138–140
Seminary students 138–140, 162, 167
Simmel, Georg 33
Simplicity principle 171
Singapore 83
Small church 67, 141
Small groups 54–56, 144, 161
Sodom and Gomorrah 101–103, 108
Southern Baptist Convention 78, 139
South Main Baptist Church, Houston 73, 94
Special purpose church 91, 92
Spiritual base 49, 50, 169
Spiritual growth 53, 133
Spiritual renewal 96
Stratification 34, 115
Storefront church 59, 60, 67, 142
Suburbs 25–27, 142
Suburban church 59, 60, 69, 79, 93–95
Sucker growth 121
Successism 131
Support system 151, 152
Sunday school 71, 153
Survey 158, 159, 167

Tallowood Baptist Church, Houston 93, 94
Teaching 44, 50, 71
Technology 23, 35, 39, 40, 51, 52
Television 24, 39, 40, 97, 160

Theological principle 169
Theological weakness 13–16, 121–
    132, 146
Third Baptist Church, San Fran-
    cisco 68
Timing principle 171
Too rapid growth 121
Tower of Babel 101, 103, 109
Tract, the 38, 161
Training 137, 159, 160, 166, 167
Transitional
    area 17–19, 26
    church 18, 77–79, 95, 96, 145–
    152

Urban exodus, so called 23, 24
Urban form 13, 24–26, 72, 142, 158
Urban social characteristics 13, 24,
    26–28, 31–35, 111–120
Urban waves of history, the 21–23
Urbanization of man 21
Unhealthy growth 121, 122, 124,
    125, 130–132
Union Baptist Association (Texas)
    73–74

Uptown (secondary business dis-
    trict) 142
Uptown church 60, 61, 63, 64, 73,
    74, 94
University church 65, 66

Village church 58, 85

Wagner, C. Peter 59, 60, 122, 124–
    126, 130, 131
Walnut Street Baptist Church,
    Louisville 96
West Memorial Baptist Church,
    Houston 94, 95
William Carey Library 136
Willow Meadows Baptist Church,
    Houston 93, 95
Wirth, Louis 32, 33
Wolf, Tom 131, 150
Worship 45, 50, 54, 56, 118, 165

Yoido Island Full Gospel Central
    Church, Seoul 87, 88, 95, 162
Yung Nak Presbyterian Church,
    Seoul 86, 87